A FIELD GUIDE TO THE APOCALYPSE

A Mostly Serious Guide to
Surviving Our Wild Times

ATHENA AKTIPIS

Illustrations by Neil Smith

Workman Publishing ✧ New York, NY

Workman
Workman Publishing
Hachette Book Group, Inc.
1290 Avenue of the Americas
New York, NY 10104
workman.com

Workman is an imprint of Workman Publishing, a division of Hachette
Book Group, Inc. The Workman name and logo are registered trademarks
of Hachette Book Group, Inc.

Design by Rae Ann Spitzenberger
Illustrations by Neil Smith
Cover image credits: (asteroid on cover, spine, and interior) Martial Red
/ Shutterstock; (stick figures on cover) Leremy / Shutterstock; (volcano on
cover) Neil Smith

The publisher is not responsible for websites (or their content) that are
not owned by the publisher.

Workman books may be purchased in bulk for business, educational,
or promotional use. For information, please contact your local bookseller
or the Hachette Book Group Special Markets Department at special.
markets@hbgusa.com.

Library of Congress Cataloging-in-Publication Data is available.

ISBN 978-1-5235-1825-8
First Edition April 2024
Printed in Malaysia on responsibly sourced paper.

10 9 8 7 6 5 4 3 2 1

CONTENTS

INTRODUCTION

Welcome to the apocalypse! You might not realize it, but as you've been going about your life, the world has been sliding into an apocalyptic state. From COVID to wildfires to climate change, it's becoming increasingly clear that we're all kinds of fucked. Species are endangered, large-scale human cooperation is waning, and many of us feel like we can't plan for the future because there's too much uncertainty about what things will be like in six months, six years, or six decades.

But don't worry, I'm here to tell you that everything is fine. We've been coping with apocalypses since the dawn of humanity—and we actually already have the tools to deal with the risks and hazards we're facing. The problem is most of us are too scared by the prospect of future catastrophes, or too traumatized by past disasters, to fully bring our brains to the table and deal with the apocalyptic moment in which we're living. This is where *A Field Guide to the Apocalypse* comes in.

In this book, I will cover the many benefits of facing and embracing the apocalypse, from peace of mind (yes, considering the end of the world can reduce your anxiety!) to the continued survival of yourself and your loved ones to actually reducing the chances that life on Earth will cease to exist. Along the way, we'll learn how to make this whole apocalypse thing fun—by integrating it into your life in ways that make it richer, more exciting, and ultimately less stressful. Instead of being paralyzed by fear, we can learn to channel our energy into excitement about the challenge of facing the world's end—and into preparation for the many reckonings we'll likely face in the coming decades.

Before we jump in, you might be wondering: Who are you? And why did you write a book about the apocalypse? The simple answer is that I am a professor who thought it would be fun to

Hi, I'm Athena, your uke-playin', science-lovin', proud-preppin', professor tour guide.

write a book about the end of the world. The apocalypse is a very serious topic, but that doesn't mean we have to take ourselves too seriously while we figure out what to do about it. Not only will having some fun make it easier to deal with all the crappy crap going on in the world right now and likely coming our way in the future, I believe that having some fun with the apocalypse is the only way for us to effectively work together to make things better.

I've come to this conclusion after more than a decade of studying human behavior in times of crisis, programming computer models of the evolution of cooperation, and organizing actual humans in dozens of conferences, workshops, and other events dedicated to solving problems. But the true roots of my interest in apocalypse mitigation began when I was a young teen living in the progress-loving, capitalism-embracing, technology-gonna-solve-all-the-problems nineties. (So, yeah, I enjoyed purchasing cassette singles and buying skirts with too many zippers at the mall.) But I also had a nagging feeling that something wasn't right in the world, that how we were living might not be the best for us and our collective future. So I started reading—a lot. I biked over to my local bookstore and read everything I could about the environment, ecology, evolutionary biology, and human psychology. I came to the conclusion that the world was kinda messed up and getting worse, and that understanding human behavior was the best place to start if we wanted to do something about it.

Over the last decade, I've started two new conferences (The International Society for Evolution, Ecology and Cancer Conference, and The Zombie Apocalypse Medicine Meeting), launched two Livestream channels (Channel Zed: The World's

Leading Zombie Apocalypse Channel, and The Cooperation Science Network), and produced and hosted four seasons of my podcast, *Zombified*. I've also directed or co-directed a bunch of projects and initiatives, including the Human Generosity Project, which is a transdisciplinary effort to look at cooperation across small-scale societies around the world, in the lab, and through computer models.

Currently, I work as an intensely interdisciplinary professor at what is possibly the most interdisciplinary university in the world: Arizona State University (ASU). I get to spend my days thinking interdisciplinary thoughts to try to solve both deep theoretical problems (like, how does cooperation evolve? Why does cancer exist? How did life arise from non-life?) and ridiculously complicated practical problems (such as, how do we get humans to cooperate on a large scale? Can we keep cancer under control using evolutionary biology? How do we prevent the end of life as we know it?). I've spent a good portion of the last decade understanding cancer from an evolutionary and cooperation theory perspective, working out how cancer cheats in the cellular cooperation that is fundamental to multicellular life, and figuring out what the implications are for cancer prevention and treatment. That work led to my first book, *The Cheating Cell: How Evolution Helps Us Understand and Treat Cancer* (2020). It turns out that cancer is a fundamental part of multicellular life, and that we (and all forms of multicellular life) are actually pretty damn good at keeping it at bay. So cancer doesn't actually have to be as depressing as it might seem!

And that's how I feel about the apocalypse. Like cancer, the apocalypse doesn't have to be a downer—it can be a lens through which we see our shared humanity, a tool for coming together and getting on the same page about our world and how to make it better.

So *what* am I, exactly? A psychologist? (I *am* in a psychology department, after all.) An evolutionary biologist? (Arguably my most important published works are about evolutionary biology.) A cancer biologist? (My last book was on that topic, after all.) Or a zombie apocalypse expert? (I've certainly spent an outsize amount of time over the last five years on zombies and the apocalypse.)

What holds together all the work I've done and the diverse approaches and methods I've used is this: Everything has to do with cooperation and conflict. So if a label is necessary, I would call myself a cooperation theorist. I employ psychology, evolutionary biology, ecology, computer science, anthropology, and many more disciplines in my work. Because I have had the time to understand human nature through these different disciplinary lenses, I'm in the ideal position to return to the issues and questions that motivated my teenage self to study evolution and behavior.

That's the point of this book—to make the apocalypse something we want to engage with and think about and tell stories around.

And those would be: Are we totally fucked? And, if so, how do we start to unfuck ourselves and the world?

You want and need somebody like me working on this problem: Somebody who uses lots of different methods and approaches to understand the world, who talks to everyone and anyone, and who is not afraid of the apocalypse, zombie or otherwise. And I need you: your curious brain, your serious-not-serious mindset, and your

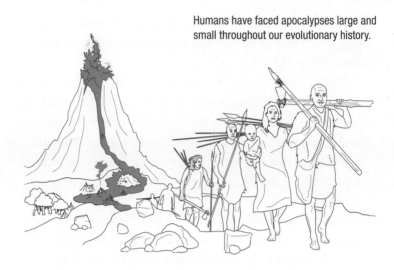

Humans have faced apocalypses large and small throughout our evolutionary history.

fun-loving and prosocial attitude about our apocalyptic times. But the truth is we all need each other. Not just to talk to about the apocalypse, but to work together to do something about the scary-as-fuck future that we are collectively facing. And to hopefully have some fun in the process.

That's the point of this book—to make the apocalypse something we want to engage with and think about and tell stories around. This helps us not just psychologically deal with the predicament we are in, but ultimately be better prepared to survive and thrive no matter what kind of apocalypse comes our way.

In the pages that follow, I'll explain what we all need to know about human nature in order to deal with other humans—and ourselves—in an array of different apocalyptic scenarios. From denial to cheating to image management to dealing with risk, I'll tackle the thorny psychological issues that crop up in so-called end times. We'll go back in history to look at how humans have dealt with apocalypses—and the uncertainty that they bring—since the dawn of time. Hunter-gatherers and other people living in small-scale societies still have to deal with lots of day-to-day and year-to-year risks that most of us living in market-integrated Western societies don't have to consider. As a result, they have valuable lessons for those of us in the developed West about how to manage serious risks and how to make this risk management a meaningful part of our lives. We'll learn from them, and then learn how to scale these risk-management capabilities to the crazy, wicked, massive scale that we are dealing with now.

Yes, this book is about things being fine, even though we're fucked. But don't get me wrong, just because we're fucked doesn't mean we should throw our collective hands up in the air and say "fuck it." We have to face reality without a fear mindset, then leverage our awesome human abilities to communicate, cooperate, and have fun to manage our risks together. Less "Fuck it, let's party," and more "Let's party and unfuck it."

At its heart, *A Field Guide to the Apocalypse* is an empowerment book that will take you from feeling fear about the uncertainty of the future to feeling ready to restructure your life to create a more sustainable and resilient future for all humankind. That sounds grand, I know. But deep down, all of us want to save the world. And if we can do that by embracing the upside of the apocalypse, so much the better. Let's get started!

THE APOCALYPSE IS UPON US AND IT'S OKAY

01

Let's start at the end. Do you have vague anxiety about the end of the world? Do you think about how the sun will eventually engulf the Earth in a giant supernova? Are you frightened that massive wildfires or biblical floods will threaten your family and destroy your home? Do you feel like maybe we got off easy with the COVID-19 pandemic—and that something much worse may be lurking in the future?

Congratulations: You're probably right!

The fact is, many of the potential disasters we'll face in the future—asteroids, volcanoes, alien invasions, pandemics, famines, floods, nuclear war—are very unlikely to happen in a given year. They are "black swans," highly improbable but often highly impactful events. If we take all the weird and unlikely ways the world might end, they add up to something frighteningly big. Even more frightening is the specter of what I call a clusterfuck apocalypse: a bunch of relatively mild or moderate catastrophes compounding upon one another, increasing the likelihood of even more bad shit happening as they unfold in concert (see page 125). So, yeah, it's likely that we're in for an apocalyptic future.

> The reality is we're not just in for an apocalyptic future, we also live in an apocalyptic present.

But the reality is we're not just in for an apocalyptic future, we also live in an apocalyptic present. We're facing a series of reckonings right now, from pandemics to climate change to the

Asteroids

Are we all going to die because of an asteroid impact? In 2004, there was a brief scare that the asteroid 99942 Apophis had a 2.7 percent chance of hitting Earth on April 13, 2029. Further calculations put the probability so low that there is no longer any concern that it will hit our planet. But that was scary.

So, do we still have to worry about asteroids? Asteroids and comets enter the Earth's atmosphere all the time, at which point we call them meteors (or shooting stars, if you're around a campfire staring up at the night sky). Most of them never impact the ground, instead burning up (or exploding) in our atmosphere on their way down. The frequency of impact events decreases as the diameter of the asteroid increases. (That means: The bigger they are, the less frequent they are, so there are lots of small ones and not many big ones.) Every 500,000 years or so we experience an impact from a meteor about 1 km in diameter. Larger ones, like the 10+ km meteor that caused the Cretaceous-Paleogene extinction event sixty-six million years ago that wiped out the dinosaurs, happen more rarely still. Nevertheless, even relatively small meteors that don't directly impact Earth can still cause massive damage. In 2013, the Chelyabinsk meteor exploded over Russia, releasing as much energy as the atomic bomb dropped on Hiroshima, Japan, in World War II, injuring more than one thousand people.

How to do a back-of-the-envelope calculation of the risk of meteor impact based on the size of the meteor:

$$\text{Frequency} = 1 \, / \, \text{diameter}^3$$

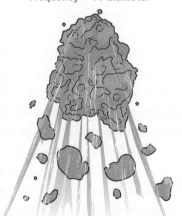

technopocalypse (i.e., smartphones hijacking our brains, social media algorithms setting the political agenda, artificial intelligence getting smarter than we are). We're all trying to survive in our own ways, whether we're adjusting how we live and work because of a pandemic, grappling with the realities of housing and food insecurity, or dealing with the devastation and environmental destruction that wildfires and other disasters wreak.

Our current moment is apocalyptic, but the worst is surely yet to come. So, what do we do about it? Should we panic, lose our shit, and go down in a massive anxiety attack? Or get all fatalistic and just eat as much sushi as we can before the oceans are empty? Or *maybe* we should look at our current apocalyptic moment as an opportunity to learn and shore up our vulnerabilities so that we can survive and thrive in these increasingly apocalyptic times?

If you're at least considering the third option as a means to deal with our pending catastrophic future, read on.

Everything Is Fine!

Now is a rough time, no question. But also, everything is fine. I don't mean it's okay that fires are raging, that climate change is accelerating, or that people around the world are dying from infectious diseases. I mean that we have to be okay with the way things are right now so that we can face reality, including our vulnerabilities, and work together to reduce the likelihood and intensity of future disasters. If we simply look the other way and pretend it's not happening, it's just going to get worse. This is not a "keep calm and carry on" kind of deal.

This is a "keep calm, face the facts, and change how you carry on" situation. And being okay with how things are is the first step.

It is hard to live with the existential risk that we're constantly facing these days. It is also tempting to ignore it, to distract ourselves, and pretend that things are fine and we aren't living in the middle of a full-on planetary crisis. But here's the thing: We don't have to *pretend* that things are fine. We can just face our apocalyptic reality and realize that we

YOU SAY YOU WANT A REVOLUTION?

We are capable—individually and collectively—of drastically changing how we do things to adapt to new threats and opportunities. This is both baked into us through evolution (see variability selection, page 30) and is apparent from our history. When systems no longer work or new circumstances alter our ability to make a living, we humans can dramatically change how we do things. The key to all of these revolutions was the hope for something better that encouraged people to take advantage of new opportunities. Now we need a revolution to protect future generations from a shitty fate. To do that, we must look at the challenge together as an exciting opportunity so that we can put our collective energy toward changing the trajectory of our future for the better.

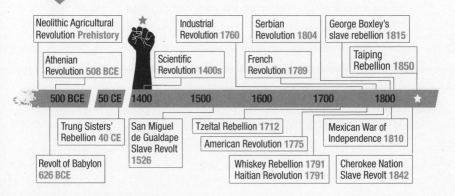

Neolithic Agricultural Revolution **Prehistory**

Athenian Revolution **508 BCE**

Industrial Revolution **1760**

Scientific Revolution **1400s**

Serbian Revolution **1804**

French Revolution **1789**

George Boxley's slave rebellion **1815**

Taiping Rebellion **1850**

500 BCE **50 CE** **1400** **1500** **1600** **1700** **1800**

Trung Sisters' Rebellion **40 CE**

Revolt of Babylon **626 BCE**

San Miguel de Gualdape Slave Revolt **1526**

Tzeltal Rebellion **1712**

American Revolution **1775**

Whiskey Rebellion **1791**
Haitian Revolution **1791**

Mexican War of Independence **1810**

Cherokee Nation Slave Revolt **1842**

actually *can* live a fulfilling life even while facing the reality of risk that exists in the world. Also, I'm happy to report that there are lots of simple things we can do to reduce our individual and collective risk of death, disease, dismemberment, and other disastrous fates.

You've probably noticed by now that I'm throwing around the words "apocalypse" and "apocalyptic" like they're household terms. That might be startling to some, though maybe you are already on board, nodding along. These past few years of pandemic panic, wicked wildfires, and wild weather have made the apocalypse a common topic at family dinners. But what does it really mean to say we're living in an apocalypse? What *is* an apocalypse anyway?

In this book, I define apocalypse not just as the end of times, but also as a revelation of the risk inherent in the world and in our lives. It is a situation that allows us to see what our vulnerabilities are and presents us with the opportunity to restructure our collective lives and mindsets to be better prepared for an uncertain future.

The word *apocalypse* comes from ancient Greek, meaning "uncover" or "reveal"—to show us an underlying reality that was previously hidden. And that reality is filled with much

more risk than we would like to believe. In this book, we'll look squarely at what makes up the risk that we all face. We'll also look at the barriers—psychological, cultural, economic, and technological—that get in the way of us both seeing it and doing something about it.

Beyond the revelation of risk, an apocalypse is also fundamentally about disaster, damage, and destruction. Some apocalypses are truly world ending; others just force a reckoning, making it necessary for us to rethink our assumptions. An apocalypse can also be the heralding of a new era, ushering in the sense that "times have changed" or that we are living in "new times." They say what doesn't kill you makes you stronger, but really it would be better to say what doesn't kill you gives you an opportunity to learn and do better next time.

Apocalypse
A catastrophic event that reveals the underlying risk that we face; an event that forces a reckoning and restructuring of the world as we know it.

Disasters are bad, no question. But in some ways, they're better than calm wonderfulness because they reveal the risk inherent in the world. And we're better off knowing those risks than keeping our heads in the sand. So why do we keep running away and avoiding the reality of our imminent demise? If we're going to really face the reality of how fucked up everything is, then we're going to have to make it less boring, less intimidating, and much more fun.

We're Built for This

Generally speaking, the apocalypse is kind of a downer. If you pick up a typical book about the end of the world, you'll quickly find yourself depressed by the future prospects of humanity

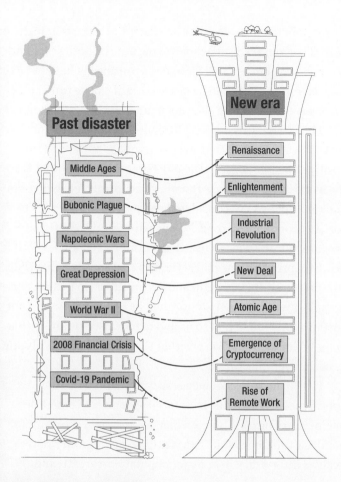

THE MOTHERS OF INVENTION

Human beings are resilient and—occasionally—very smart. Historically, times of death and disaster have given rise to innovative thinking and clever inventions. The Middle Ages led to the Renaissance, the Bubonic Plague gave way to the Enlightenment, the Napoleonic Wars inspired the Industrial Revolution, and the Great Depression spawned the New Deal. Necessity is truly the neglectful mother of desperate invention.

or mired in the technicalities of existential risk assessment, or both. That approach somehow manages to be both scary and boring in one breath. But the apocalypse doesn't have to be that way. The apocalypse can be fascinating, it can be fun—hell, it can even be an exciting and super-practical lifestyle choice.

That's what this book is all about—the peace of mind that comes from adopting an apocalyptic mindset and the positive lifestyle consequences of being ready for the end of the world as we know it. After all, you can only feel truly safe and relaxed if you've considered and prepared for things to go catastrophically wrong. Being mentally and emotionally prepared for the apocalypse also requires a certain level of practical preparation, a lifestyle shift that can be radical but also personally meaningful and deeply satisfying. Mentally grappling with the apocalypse gives us a chance to figure out what is really important to us and to build a community that helps buffer us from risk, whether those risks are apocalyptic or of the everyday variety.

Here's the very good news: We are adapted for the apocalypse. We humans have faced apocalypses since the beginning of our existence, which means that we're built for handling a lot more shit than we think we can. Our brains evolved in a world where major population-threatening crises were regularly happening. We have brains full of risk-management strategies and social abilities that help us deal with catastrophic events, both on an individual and a collective societal level. Humans who couldn't deal with catastrophes didn't survive, so we come from a long evolutionary line of apocalypse-hardy humans who worked together to get through the hardest of times.

In other words, each of us has an inner apocalypse survivor, an inner prepper good at assessing risk and managing it. Unfortunately, our very Western, market-integrated lives don't leave a lot of space and time for us to embrace that inner prepper. Most of us are driven to overworking and relying on fragile supply chains for the things we need. Too often we ignore our surroundings, including both the hazards we face in our local environments as well as the opportunities we have for being more connected to the natural world that ultimately sustains and protects us all.

If you're new to prepping, you likely have some stereotypes about preppers. You might think they are all gun-obsessed former military guys who have been through some serious shit. But preppers are much more diverse than you might expect. There are mom preppers, green preppers, and intentional community-focused preppers. Many preppers are socially oriented and sustainability-focused, ready and willing to share their resources and knowledge to support

We evolved to deal with immense uncertainty, rapid change, and unexpected disasters. Indeed, our ability to understand and deal with risk is part of what makes us human.

everybody in being more prepared. Whether you know it or not, you have an inner prepper inside you too, itching to get started assessing risk and shoring up your own vulnerabilities in case of an apocalypse.

But our evolved abilities for dealing with apocalypses are not about hunkering down and avoiding everyone and everything—they are about taking in information and engaging deeply with our world and the people around us. Since the dawn of human existence, we have been assessing our world, evaluating risk, and changing our individual and collective behavior so that we're better prepared.

As you continue reading, remember: The apocalypse is upon us and it's okay. Because we're built for this. We evolved to deal with immense uncertainty, rapid change, and unexpected disasters. Indeed, our ability to understand and deal with risk is part of what makes us human.

APOCALYPSE CULTURE

Culturally speaking, the apocalypse has been center stage since the beginning of recorded history. We've probably been talking about past apocalypses, prepping for future ones, or both since we evolved to talk in the first place.

Ancient Greeks saw history as cyclical, with periods of affluence punctuated by catastrophes; Indigenous American societies including the Hopi, Seneca, and Paiute told stories about the end of the world; and prophecies of the apocalypse are sprinkled throughout the modern Christian Bible. The Ancient Maya believed in a cyclical calendar, which was grossly misinterpreted into an apocalypse calendar, prompting the 2012 phenomenon (with December 21, 2012, marking "the end" of a 5,126-year-long cycle in the Mesoamerican Long Count Calendar, known colloquially as the Mayan Calendar) in which a nontrivial portion of the world's population was earnestly preparing for the end of times.

These beliefs and expectations about the end of the world fall under the broad heading of what is called eschatology (eSS-ka-tol-ogy). Eschatology is a part of large-scale religions as well as cultural beliefs in small-scale societies. We humans have spent an awful lot of time thinking about the end of the world—look no further than the religious texts from Abrahamic (Christianity, Judaism) and Dharmic (Hinduism, Buddhism) religions. The end of the world scares us, no question, but we can't stop talking about it.

Yet talking about the end of the world can be tricky. On the one hand, it's important to get on the same page about the threats we face. But when people get too focused on and invested in a particular story about the end of the world, it can have a bizarre impact on society, leading to what economists and game theorists call endgame effects. If people think the end is nigh and there's nothing they can do about it, they might stop investing in the future and doing other tasks that help society function. But talking about the apocalypse doesn't *have* to lead to endgame effects if people feel like there's something they can do, especially if they see that everyone is invested in doing *something*. In fact, that kind of shared attention and effort on managing risk and solving problems can be hugely motivating for us super-social humans.

Managing Risk Is Part of Being Human

Before the advent of agriculture and industry, and before the infiltration of technology into every crevice of our lives, things were very different here on Earth. Life was not necessarily brutish and short, but it was pretty damn risky. If we look back at what life was like for our ancestors as they were rapidly evolving our uniquely human characteristics (from about one million to ten thousand years ago), we see that the circumstances were fairly apocalyptic. Because of

Infectious Diseases

COVID is arguably the most apocalyptic global crisis most of us have faced. But this apocalypse isn't so bad when you consider the broader context of past infectious diseases and likely future ones.

Even the flu, to which we have become pretty habituated, could easily mutate into a global-pandemic-causing virus with a far higher death toll than COVID. Experts estimate that the chance of an influenza pandemic that kills six million people in the first year is around 1 percent every year (by comparison, the COVID-19 pandemic killed between two and three million people in its first year). Pandemics have also been increasing in frequency over time. Over the next fifty years, chances are better than not that we'll see a devastating flu sweep through the world, wreaking significantly greater havoc than COVID did.

Influenza is not the only possible future pandemic. Something else could broadside us like COVID. It's pretty damn hard to estimate the chance of another novel infectious agent like COVID, but it's clear the risks of pandemics are going up. A full 75 percent of emerging infectious diseases are zoonotic, meaning that they come from nonhuman animals. Since the advent of agriculture and industry, we humans have been encroaching further and further into the habitats of other animals, making transmission of diseases from animals to humans more likely. And we have much larger and denser populations than we've ever had in human history, with the ability to move between them faster than ever before.

And let's not forget about the deadliest zoonotic diseases: vector-borne diseases. Vector-borne diseases are transmitted among humans (or other animals) through blood-sucking creatures like mosquitoes, fleas, ticks, and lice. Since the vectors don't get sick from the disease, they're able to keep transmitting it no matter how deadly it is (as with mosquito-transmitted malaria).

the eccentricities of Earth's orbit at the time, the climate was changing rapidly. This could mean that an area with a lot of rainfall and vegetation when your grandparents were young would be dried up and barren by the time you were an adult. As a result, we humans have been evolutionarily selected to recover from disasters and quickly adapt to new situations (a process called variability selection, see page 30). And really this has been happening since the beginning of human existence, as we've had to deal with epic droughts, floods, famines, erupting volcanoes, earthquakes, and more.

These risks from environmental variability were something humans faced mostly over the scale of generations, but if we break it down in terms of average risk over the course of our typical ancestor's lifetime, it's astounding how much death and destruction was part of daily life for hunter-gatherers. During much of human evolutionary history,

somewhere between 20 and 30 percent of your social group would die from a catastrophic event in your lifetime. These deaths often happened as a result of natural disasters, wars, famine, or disease. Some human populations dealt with much bigger risks as well, as they migrated thousands of miles across uncertain territory to colonize the globe.

And really, it's our ability to understand and manage risk that makes us human. Compared to any other species on Earth, we are by far the best at processing information, identifying

A BRIEF HISTORY OF RISK MANAGEMENT

Making a living as a human being on Earth has always been risky. During our time on this planet, we have had many different strategies for getting food and managing the risk of sometimes not having enough.

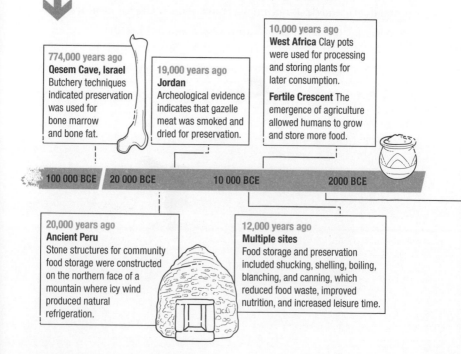

10,000 years ago
West Africa Clay pots were used for processing and storing plants for later consumption.

Fertile Crescent The emergence of agriculture allowed humans to grow and store more food.

774,000 years ago
Qesem Cave, Israel
Butchery techniques indicated preservation was used for bone marrow and bone fat.

19,000 years ago
Jordan
Archeological evidence indicates that gazelle meat was smoked and dried for preservation.

100 000 BCE — 20 000 BCE — 10 000 BCE — 2000 BCE

20,000 years ago
Ancient Peru
Stone structures for community food storage were constructed on the northern face of a mountain where icy wind produced natural refrigeration.

12,000 years ago
Multiple sites
Food storage and preservation included shucking, shelling, boiling, blanching, and canning, which reduced food waste, improved nutrition, and increased leisure time.

risks, and then setting up systems and plans and contingencies to buffer ourselves from those risks. If we look at how small-scale societies operate today (our best guess for how our human ancestors lived), we see that a lot of practices revolve around managing risk—whether it's the risk of not finding enough tubers when you go out digging or the chance your livestock dies in an apocalyptic winter storm.

In my work as co-director of the Human Generosity Project, I have seen firsthand the diverse strategies that humans have in our collective toolbox for dealing with risk. The first one is called risk retention, which is basically when you insure yourself by having enough resources to get through hard times

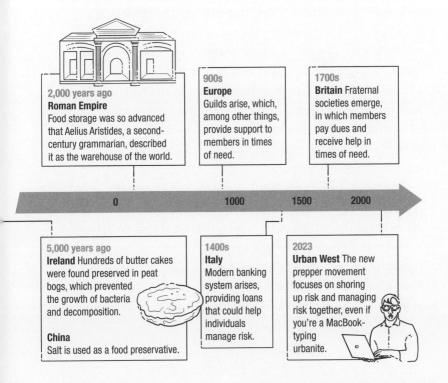

2,000 years ago
Roman Empire
Food storage was so advanced that Aelius Aristides, a second-century grammarian, described it as the warehouse of the world.

900s
Europe
Guilds arise, which, among other things, provide support to members in times of need.

1700s
Britain Fraternal societies emerge, in which members pay dues and receive help in times of need.

0   1000   1500   2000

5,000 years ago
Ireland Hundreds of butter cakes were found preserved in peat bogs, which prevented the growth of bacteria and decomposition.

China
Salt is used as a food preservative.

1400s
Italy
Modern banking system arises, providing loans that could help individuals manage risk.

2023
Urban West The new prepper movement focuses on shoring up risk and managing risk together, even if you're a MacBook-typing urbanite.

(like having enough livestock so you're not totally screwed if some of them die from disease). This strategy works great if you have plenty of resources. But if you don't, simply avoiding risk is an option: Not doing things that put you at risk is a solid, if unglamorous, strategy. But not everyone has the ability to simply avoid risks, because most of the ways we make a living as humans (ancestral or modern) involve some measure of risk.

If you can't self-insure or avoid risk, you're left with two choices: reducing your risk or sharing it. Sharing risk is probably the most important (and definitely the most social) form of risk management that we humans do. To share risk, you obviously need other people who want to do the same. In the societies we've studied in the Human Generosity Project, risk sharing (technically "risk transfer" or "risk pooling") is rampant. Across societies, people ask each other for help when they are in need, and their partners respond by helping them without expecting anything in return. These systems of mutual aid go by different names—osotua among Maasai, kerekere among Fijians, neighboring in the American West—but they all share the same function of helping buffer individuals from the risks of trying to make a living in an uncertain environment.

As this book unfolds, we'll see just how critical our social lives are to managing risk, and why having a solid community is key to dealing with looming and actual disasters. We'll learn how our abilities to assess and manage risk have allowed us to face hazards and uncertainty with equanimity and resilience throughout human history, and how we can learn from these strategies to better deal with the challenges and risks inherent in our modern lives.

TOP 5 LESSONS FROM PAST APOCALYPSES

1 We come from a long line of humans who survived (and thrived) through catastrophes.

2 Apocalypse prep is built into our evolutionary and cultural DNA.

3 Managing risk and building community are key to surviving apocalypses.

4 Telling stories about the end of the world can be fun, but also can lead to weird and counterproductive prepping if it's not based on true knowledge about risk.

5 The apocalypse doesn't have to be the end of the world; it can be the beginning of a new era.

The way that we manage risk changed somewhat after agriculture came on the scene about ten thousand years ago. Life became less risky in some ways and riskier in others. Farming meant we could grow food, so we were no longer dependent on foraging and hunting for having enough to eat on a day-to-day basis. This also meant that we weren't as dependent on others for help if we didn't find enough food on a given day. While agriculture allowed us to grow food, store it, and self-insure, it also led to us dealing with risk individually more often instead of relying on help from others if we fell short.

Agriculture also meant that populations grew, the nutritional quality of diets went down, and the chance of large-scale famine went way up. If crops failed because of bad weather, insect swarms, or plant diseases, the consequences could be catastrophic. Less food plus more mouths to feed as populations continued to grow also meant situations where everybody was likely to be in need at the same time.

This is what happened during the Irish potato famine in the mid-1800s. Everybody was growing potatoes—and mostly just one species of potato. So when potato blight—caused by a microorganism called *Phytophthora infestans*—started infecting potatoes in Ireland, it destroyed the crop everyone depended on for food. This contributed to an almost decade-long famine and the death of about a million people—certainly an apocalypse by the standards we're using here.

Agriculture and industry helped us manage some risks, but they also introduced new risks and—critically—changed the scale of the risks we faced. Rather than dealing with more local challenges, such as collecting enough food from hunting and gathering near your camp, we began to face massively correlated shocks, including country-wide famines, global pandemics, and worldwide economic depressions.

We haven't evolved to deal with risks that play out on a massive scale, especially the kinds that could cause the absolute end of the world versus "just" a local catastrophe. And that's part of why we are so fucked right now. But here's the thing: With an understanding of our evolutionary limitations for managing risk, we will actually be in a much better place to deal with the large, existential risks we face. We already have the ability to deal with risk on a local scale—what we need to do now is scale up those strategies to the right level.

Because, in one sense, these aren't particularly special times. But also, these *are* special times because we've gotten

> We already have the ability to deal with risk on a local scale—what we need to do now is scale up those strategies to the right level.

WICKED PROBLEMS AND CLUSTERFUCK APOCALYPSES

We are facing a multitude of challenges that are deeply entangled with one another. Some of these problems are set in motion by other problems in falling-domino fashion. For example, wildfires alter soils, which can then increase landslide and flooding risk. Other problems are self-reinforcing cycles, like pandemics that put strain on our health-care system, which then can worsen the very pandemics we're trying to manage.

ourselves into wicked trouble. The increasing scale and entanglement of risk in our modern world means that we need new and clever strategies to manage those risks.

The good news is a lot of us are ready for something new. We've been asking ourselves some uncomfortable questions over the past few years: Why the fuck are we all going to work every day, sending our kids to school, buying so much stuff we don't need on Amazon, and paying more and more for increasingly bad lattes? Should we do something different? If so, what?

Considering these questions—and proposing solutions—is what this book is about. We'll look at what we can do differently, individually and collectively, now that the apocalypse is actually a thing that we have to grapple with in our day-to-day lives— not to mention the prospects of utter catastrophic disasters looming over our collective heads. The good news? It will be fun. The bad news? You'll have to reexamine a lot of assumptions you've probably lived with your whole life, including what you actually need, what you don't need, what friends are for, and most importantly, how vulnerable you (and all of us) are to The Big One.

YOUR BRAIN ON THE APOCALYPSE

02

What's the one thing you'd want to have on you at all times in the apocalypse? A weapon? Duct tape? An emergency blanket? A pack of cards? Some whiskey? Cold hard cash?

Me? I'd choose brains. And you should too. No matter what you have in your go-bag—the things you'd absolutely take with you when fleeing in an emergency—if you don't have your brains, frankly, you're screwed. And considering that many of us lose our minds even when the apocalypse *isn't* raging in our immediate vicinity, keeping it together mentally when shit hits the fan can be a serious challenge.

We need a new set of tools to survive and thrive as we face this unknown apocalyptic future. You can pack your go-bag with a first aid kit, an emergency blanket, a LifeStraw (or water purification tablets), emergency rations, and matches, but if you're not mentally ready for a disaster, all that stuff will do you no good. This chapter is another tool for your go-bag: a tool for your mind.

Our brains are unequivocally the most valuable assets we have in the apocalypse. They house our knowledge, know-how, and skills. Not only is your brain crucial to your survival, it's a solid investment when things get dicey. Your brain isn't like the other stuff in your go-bag—no one can take it away from you and it's no good to somebody else if you're dead (except maybe to a peckish zombie).

> Our brains are unequivocally the most valuable assets we have in the apocalypse.

The right mental mindset is nonnegotiable when it comes to dealing with the apocalypse. But don't worry, I'm not going to tell you to stop doom-scrolling and meditate (though that probably won't hurt). I'm here to let you know that there's another way to get through the apocalypse. Just get right in there and take it head-on, dammit! We have to look it in the eerily unfeeling eye, face it with our best posture, wrap our collective minds around it, and take on our fucked-up world like an enthusiastic Woodstock cleanup crew.

But to do that, we need to have our brains in the right place. Only then can we adapt to this new day and age, working with the new information and our new reality as it reveals itself, instead of fighting against it.

When I tell people that I'm writing a book about how the apocalypse is upon us and it's okay, they almost always assume it's a book about hope and optimism, a smiling-while-the-world-crashes-down-around-us approach. Yes, there's a certain kind of optimism in these pages, a grounded sense of hope that we can and will make it through the apocalyptic challenges we face with our humanity intact. But more than hope or optimism, this book is about facts—that, while the world is basically going to hell while we Instacart and retweet, we already have the skills and abilities we need to deal with it.

Brains, Brains, Brains!

Inside that head of yours is about three pounds of neurons, support cells, and blood vessels that make up one of the most complex information-processing machines in the known universe: your brain. It is only about 2 percent of your total weight, but it plays a hugely outsize role in who you are. Which makes sense, of course: If you were to (God forbid) lose an arm or a leg, you'd be pretty broken up about it. If you were to lose your brain, however, there'd no longer be a you to care about it. Your brain plays an important role in keeping you alive and functioning—no small feat—but it also houses all the unique traits that make you who you are as a person, as an individual. Without it, you'd be nothing more than a lump of purposeless cells and organs, with no hope for survival—both because there'd be no brain to hope and because none of us can survive without a brain.

Our brains play a ridiculously big role in regulating many of the systems in our bodies, though they're not the whole story when it comes to understanding how and why we respond to the world. They're more like the tip of a neuronal iceberg—one that reaches down your spinal cord, around your viscera, through your limbs, and along every inch of your skin. Your brain sends and receives messages along the neuronal superhighway that is your nervous system. Your brain is also part of a wildly complex signaling system involving dozens of neurotransmitters and hormones (including familiar ones like dopamine, oxytocin, cortisol, and adrenaline/epinephrine) that regulate brain function and communicate with the rest of your body.

Anatomically speaking, our brains are really just a glorified bundle of nerves sitting at the top of our spinal cords. And nerves are just cells specialized for transmitting signals. But really all cells in our bodies process information, both inside the cells themselves and in communication with other cells. Cells can also process and send information to other cells electrically, by changing their polarization.

Using electricity to send information inside multicellular bodies was a super-important evolutionary innovation because it is *so much faster* than producing molecules and then having those molecules bounce around until they find a receptor on a neighboring cell. What makes our brains so cool is that they're made of huge numbers of cells that are specialized for sending super-fast signals. And when you put that many rapid-fire signal transmission units together, you get a hell of a lot of information-processing potential.

Our brains and the rest of our bodies are in unimaginably tight and constant communication. This happens via super-fast neural pathways (at a rate of about 200 miles per hour), slightly slower neurotransmitter pathways, and painfully slow hormonal pathways (hormones take minutes to diffuse into the bloodstream). If we want to understand how and why we respond to apocalyptic stress, we need to understand what happens to both our bodies and our brains when confronted with possible threats.

That self-important bouquet of about a trillion very special cells that we call our brains is there because processing power—and the ability to process quickly—is a pretty good tool for staying alive, not to mention passing one's genes on to the next generation. In fact, our brains (plus the rest of our bodies) are constantly processing huge amounts of information below our conscious awareness.

THE AMYGDALA OF FEAR

Deep inside your brain is a small almond-shaped bundle of neurons called the amygdala, which is responsible for a hell of a lot of the unpleasant feelings you've had over the years. The function of the amygdala, a collection of neurons that processes information from the outside world, is to make a "decision" (without you consciously realizing it) about whether or not you're facing a threat. If it decides there's a threat, you feel fear; if it decides there is not a threat, you feel fine.

The amygdala is responsible for the fears most of us are born with (e.g., snakes, spiders, heights), as well as those we learn over the course of our lives. What we feel as fear is, in information-processing terms, downstream from the amygdala. It comes from a combination of neural signals, hormones, and neurotransmitters that flood our systems when the amygdala does the neuronal equivalent of pulling the fire alarm. When that happens, your body actually reacts to a kind of fire, drenching itself with a spray of sprinklers in the form of hormones and neurotransmitters that help us do useful things in the face of danger.

PRIMAL DANGER

We're not alone in possessing amygdalas—all mammals have them. Birds and reptiles have what's called amygdala homologs, structures similar to the amygdala that perform the same function of regulating fear behaviors and helping protect them from danger. If we look deeper, even the simplest forms of life have systems to protect them from harm—neural alarm systems that process information and help them preserve their lives.

Being able to tell the difference between danger and not danger is really important. In evolutionary biology, it's what we call an adaptive problem, and it is one that has life-or-death (or other serious) consequences. So organisms that are good at solving these problems are more likely to pass on their genes than those that are not.

"Simpler" organisms—with less information-processing neural matter—have fear systems that function on more limited information from their active world and their history of experiences. Humans, on the other hand, do a lot more information processing, including simulating entire future scenarios in that gray matter we call our prefrontal cortex (PFC, the part of our brain involved in executive function, including planning, decision-making, and the like). When we encounter information that is ambiguous—where our amygdala can't tell if it is something dangerous or not—it gets routed through our prefrontal cortex.

If the amygdala decides there is a serious threat, the prefrontal cortex doesn't get a say before signals are routed through the body to trigger a stress response.

But here's the thing about that notorious PFC: Its role in our fear circuit is limited. If the amygdala decides there is a serious threat, the PFC doesn't get a say before signals are routed through the body to trigger a stress response. In this case, the amygdala activates the sympathetic nervous system (raising your blood pressure, speeding your heart rate, and getting you ready for some fight-or-flight action), thus suppressing your PFC. That's why it can be hard to think straight when you are super-stressed: because your amygdala made a judgment call that it was more important to get you mobilized for action than to spend time carefully weighing the proper course of action. It's not so much that your brain shuts down when there's danger—it's more like the part of your brain that does the subtle and complex context-dependent information processing (the PFC) is deprioritized.

Adapted for the Apocalypse

The truth is, we've been getting ready for the end of the world since the beginning of it, or at least since our brains evolved to the point where we were aware of the risks we faced. Since the beginning of humans, we have been experiencing little apocalypses. These events were often relatively local and small-scale compared to many of the apocalypses we face today. But in those times, before a globalized world, local catastrophes *were* the end of the world to the people affected.

Remember, during the evolutionary history of the human species (i.e., a few hundred thousand years ago when our ancestors were evolving), it's likely that 20 to 30 percent of all people died from some apocalyptic event during the typical person's lifetime, including natural disasters, wars, famine, and disease. This doesn't mean we've adapted to the point where it's easy for us to deal with catastrophes when they happen—we know that these kinds of disasters and losses can be devastatingly traumatic—but it does mean that we come from a long line of humans that dealt, one way or another, with apocalypses on a regular basis.

BUILT FOR SURVIVAL

People often talk about survivalism like it's a weird and paranoid pastime that only attracts ultra-eccentric, rural-living gun-wielders or Mason jar–stuffing back-to-the-landers. But survivalism is core to who we are as humans. And because we have had to survive some recurrently bad shit, we've evolved to be pretty apocalypse-resistant.

The first principle of evolution by natural selection is that organisms evolve to be good at surviving the environments that they experience in their evolutionary histories. It's what Herbert Spencer and Charles Darwin meant when they used the phrase "survival of the fittest." Fittest in this case means the best fit with the environment. (It does not necessarily mean the strongest, fastest, and smartest; in fact, all those characteristics can be super metabolically costly and are

HOW APOCALYPSES HAVE SHAPED HUMANITY

Whether it's a ground-shaking earthquake, a lava-spewing volcano, a parching drought, or a drenching and destructive storm, disasters have shaped us from the beginning of history. Disasters not only bring death and destruction, they can also cause long-term demographic and geographic shifts.

For example, after the eruption of Mt. Vesuvius (79 CE), survivors transformed the culture of neighboring cities. After Hurricane Katrina, upwards of 100,000 New Orleanians settled in Houston, adding to Cajun and Creole culture.

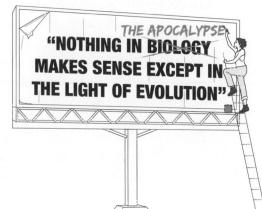

disfavored by natural selection unless they're *absolutely* necessary.)

A lot of things that are otherwise puzzling about human nature make sense when you look at them through an evolutionary lens. That's why we'll be using evolutionary biology to understand how and why we do what we do when shit starts hitting the proverbial fan.

Given our evolutionary past filled with apocalypses, we're also the product of what I call survival of the survivalists. In other words, those who were good at getting ready for apocalypses were more likely to survive them (and then reproduce!)—and help their kin do the same.

Another thing about survival of the survivalists: It doesn't just apply to the evolution of organisms via natural selection. It also applies to groups of humans and cultural evolution. Meaning: Groups of humans that have norms and rules to help them survive will in fact be more likely to survive (and reproduce!), giving them more of a chance to pass along those norms and rules than their less-savvy, noncooperative cousins.

BUILT FOR CHANGE

As humans, we've had to deal with a lot of change over lifetimes and generations. We evolved during geological periods when there was dramatic ecological change. The last million or so years have seen increasing fluctuations to our planet's climate and increasing fluctuations from large planetary cycles interweaving intensely. For example, precessional variations (like the wobble you see in a spinning top) in the Earth's orbit happen at 19,000-, 23,000- and 100,000-year intervals, and cause dramatic fluctuations in precipitation and vegetation.

When organisms live in environments that fluctuate a lot—where ecological change and catastrophes are part of life—those environments select for organisms that are good at dealing with variation and uncertainty. In evolutionary biology, this is called variability selection.

And we humans have the telltale signs of a variability-selected species. We possess very flexible eating habits and are unbelievably variable in our social organization and group size. These features allowed our ancestors to adapt to changing ecological conditions by eating new things and forming and organizing groups tailored to their changing circumstances. Our cognitive abilities, including memory, language, and social learning, may have evolved because they made it easier to survive (and thrive) as ecosystems were changing all around us. Put together, this translates as humans having a whole suite of abilities that were forged in the evolutionary fire of catastrophic conditions throughout our history as a species.

Variability Selection

The evolutionary process that selects for organisms that are able to adapt to changing situations. Environments that fluctuate dramatically over lifetimes or even generations can favor organisms that are particularly good at dealing with change.

Built to fill the cognitive niche

Although it may feel obvious, it's worth calling attention to: We humans are well adapted because we use our brains to figure out how to survive in new, challenging, and changing environments. Evolutionarily and ecologically speaking, we entered what renowned evolutionary anthropologist John Tooby calls the cognitive niche. A niche is basically an ecological environment that has certain environmental features and, in general, organisms that specialize in living in particular ecological niches, such as sandy shores or mountain treetops. According to Tooby, we humans have a niche too, but ours isn't a single ecological place—our niche is a cognitive one. Our niche is being able to use our brains to survive, often regardless of the conditions.

By taking in and processing a huge amount of information, we're able to enter new environments and figure out how to make a living, assess risks, and learn as we go. We can internalize a great deal of varied information, figure out patterns, and make (and remake) plans as our environments (and the risk inherent in them) reveal themselves to us.

Cognitive Niche
Humans have inhabited changing environments throughout our evolutionary history, forcing us to regularly migrate to new environments where we have to figure out how to shelter, find water, eat, and more. And learning how to survive in these new environments required brain power, hence evolutionary selection for genes that made for clever and adaptable brains.

Built to make babies fast

Because we evolved in a world where there was a lot of apocalyptic environmental change as well as migration to new places with resources, we were evolutionarily selected to reproduce quickly when conditions were good. The human potential for having babies is far greater than what would be necessary to replace ourselves, which serves as a sort of evolutionary insurance plan for the apocalypse. When resources are plentiful, even women in small-scale societies who breastfeed for a few years can have a baby every three to

ANATOMY OF AN APOCALYPTIC BADASS

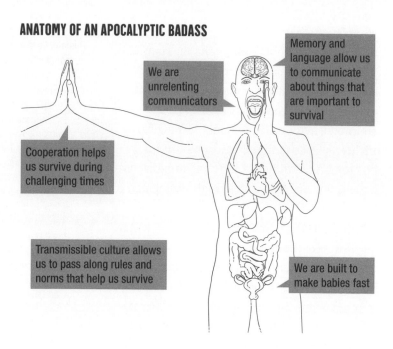

Memory and language allow us to communicate about things that are important to survival

We are unrelenting communicators

Cooperation helps us survive during challenging times

Transmissible culture allows us to pass along rules and norms that help us survive

We are built to make babies fast

four years. Assuming a roughly twenty-year reproductive life, that's a potential for about six babies on average. Way more than replacement levels.

But here's the catch: To actually achieve a fast rate of reproduction—a kind of medium-term apocalypse resilience—humans had to depend on each other for help, or at least on those in their social circles. Based on our best guesses from current hunter-gatherers, kids don't start being able to sustain themselves from their own foraging until around age eleven. This means that offspring needed to be provisioned not just by their parents, but also by others in the community if their parents had several children at once. This means that part of our apocalypse resilience is fundamentally social. Among modern Western, market-integrated humans, some children don't start being able to sustain themselves economically until they are well into their twenties or even their thirties. So, it's probably a good thing that most of us don't have upward of six children each.

Built to communicate

Not only are humans avid cooperators, we're also unrelenting communicators. We actively teach skills, share knowledge, and tell stories that can help us survive and thrive when we face challenges and catastrophes.

For example, in small-scale societies, the elderly are often the repositories of information that can be critical for the survival of the whole community when things get tough. Adults and elders teach subsistence skills to young people, including how to make a bow and arrow for hunting, where to forage for tubers, or how to climb a tree to get delicious high-calorie honey without falling out of said tree, getting bee stings, or some combination of the two. This ability to share information from generation to generation might've even shaped the evolution of our long life spans, as elders could contribute to the well-being of future generations after they were past their reproductive years. Since humans in small-scale societies typically lived in groups made up of genetic kin or among people who were highly interdependent with one another for survival and reproduction, sharing information wasn't just a good idea on a human level for their social bonds, but also as a strategy that made evolutionary sense.

Volcanoes

About one thousand years ago (1086 CE), there was a volcanic eruption near human settlements just a few miles north of what is now Flagstaff, Arizona (where I live at the moment). That very likely sucked for everyone living nearby when it happened, but in the long-term it was actually a good thing for the local population because the resulting volcanic soils were richer and people could grow more food going forward. Ultimately—and ironically—the region was able to support a larger population after the volcanic eruption than before it.

That volcanic eruption generated Sunset Crater, which is now an extinct volcano, so I'm not in any immediate danger. But I am living in a geological hot spot (known as the San Francisco volcanic field, which is nowhere near the city of San Francisco) that has volcanic

Last major eruption 1854
VEI 3
Immediate deaths ~80,000
Aftermath deaths ~960,000

Mount Rainier
Seattle, U.S.

Last major eruption 70,000 years ago
VEI 8
Immediate deaths ~100,000
Aftermath deaths ~165.5M, rising to 5B with ensuing global winter

Yellowstone
Wyoming, U.S.

Kīlauea
Hawaii, U.S.

Last major eruption 2023
VEI 5
Immediate deaths ~2,000
Aftermath deaths ~22M

Last major eruption 2023
VEI 0
Immediate deaths ~3,100
Aftermath deaths ~50,000

Popocatépetl
Mexico City, Mexico

eruptions every few thousand years. It's conceivable that the ground underneath me could literally shift as the North American Plate continues to move eastward, causing an eruption in one of those dormant volcanoes northeast of town. It's not likely to happen in my lifetime, but it's part of the history and the future of this place.

In fact, the possibility of volcanic eruptions is part of the risk profile of many human settlements and cities (St. Helens, anyone?) because the land around them is often more fertile, and in some places (like Iceland) they even use geothermal energy to heat homes and power industries. There's that apocalyptic upside again—at least for volcanoes. Since you still might want to avoid living near one that could apocalyptically erupt during your lifetime, here's a handy map!

Last major eruption 1538
VEI 7
Immediate deaths ~1.5M
Aftermath deaths Unknown; possible 5B with ensuing global winter

VEI Volcanic explosivity index, a logarithmic scale measuring the volume of material ejected from the volcano

Immediate deaths Deaths in days following eruption, assuming no warning (which is unlikely, but has happened)

Aftermath deaths Deaths in weeks, months, and years following eruption

Campi Flegrei
Naples, Italy

Last major eruption 2023
VEI 4
Immediate deaths ~70,000
Aftermath deaths Unknown; likely closure of trade routes, air travel, and internet connections

Mount Merapi
Java, Indonesia

Built to cooperate

Cooperation is a central feature of human life across societies. It was also a key factor in how people survived through apocalypses both large and small throughout our evolutionary history. An example of this would be people in small-scale societies who share food with those who are hungry and not able to get enough food for themselves, whether they're children, the elderly, disabled, or just unlucky.

Our willingness to help those in need is often based on the simple knowledge that we have the capacity to help and relieve the need we see (as we will see in Chapter 3). Also, when we feel interdependent with those around us, that makes it easier to help.

Now that you know a little bit about how our evolutionary history has made you into an apocalyptic badass, or at least endowed you with the potential to be one, it's time to flip to the other side of the evolutionary coin: the barriers that get in the way of us dealing with the apocalypse head-on.

We're Not in Denial

If our brains are our most valuable asset in the apocalypse, then denial is our worst vulnerability. If you don't have an accurate understanding of your abilities or limits, you can get yourself in deeper than you can handle. And if we collectively don't understand our abilities and limits, we have absolutely no hope of digging ourselves out of this mess.

Yet sadly, we are quite good at deceiving ourselves: about how awesome we are, about how kick-ass our teams are, and of course, about how viable our collective future is if we do nothing different. Self-deception can also be adaptive, particularly if your goal is to try to convince others you're a good partner or teammate, or that your company, city, or country is the best. Denial does have benefits—it can help us get through tough times when we really just need to deal with the apocalyptic situation at hand instead of turning into a hot mess of rumination. But denial can have huge costs as well, particularly if you use it as a way to avoid preparing for the reality of risk that we all face.

So how do we get to a place of balance? A place where we can be okay about the current state and future fate of the world? Facing reality is the first step toward surviving and thriving in the apocalypse. If we don't face reality but instead fight it with denial and avoidance, we can end up making ourselves more vulnerable to future disasters because we are resistant to processing and learning from the past. Luckily, there are effective psychological strategies that can help us get over our denial.

THE PROS AND CONS OF UNBRIDLED OPTIMISM

Optimism is a funny thing. On the one hand it is the source of all disappointment, but on the other, it's the font of inspiration, motivation, and excitement about the world around you. If you're feeling optimistic about what comes next in your life, you're more likely to invest in long-term goals and contribute to making a brighter future. However, optimism's dark side can mean that if you're too positive about everything, you might be less willing to think about the possible downsides or to do costly but necessary things that could reduce the likelihood of bad things happening in the future. For example, say you're super optimistic about your twelve-year-old car's viability, so you don't spend the money to get the brakes checked and the engine tuned up. You could be putting yourself at risk because you're unwilling to face the reality of your car needing a proper tune-up to keep operating safely.

UNBRIDLED OPTIMISM

PROS	CONS
• "Fake it till you make it" actually works for quite a lot of stuff.	• It's fucking annoying for everyone else who is trying to deal with reality.
• Crippling depression during the apocalypse is suboptimal.	• It discounts the fact that wallowing in doom is secretly quite enjoyable and strangely comforting.
• Optimism puts you in a better mindset to be successful.	• You miss out on how fun it can be to embrace the end of the world.
	• Too much optimism could lead to bad or hasty decisions.

The key to effective optimism is to make it conditional. In other words, we can have hope and excitement for the future *if* we do X, Y, and Z to get our collective act together to prevent things from seriously deteriorating. Apocalyptic thinking doesn't have to necessarily be a bad thing that makes us stop investing in the future. In fact, apocalyptic thinking can be a good thing sometimes, if we're doing it in a fun and social way that moves us to collective action rather than self-indulgent despair. Certain kinds of apocalyptic thinking, like imagining a climate apocalypse scenario that prompts an assessment of your local risks or watching zombie movies and imagining what you'll do when the next viral apocalypse hits, can help us engage and get over our individual and collective denial.

WHY BE IN DENIAL?

Before we relegate denial to the dumpster of useless defense mechanisms, let's take a look at what denial can (and often does) do for us. Denial wouldn't be around if it didn't—at least sometimes—serve an important function for us. Understanding that function and when it can help is a great way to understand when it cannot.

Here are some of the ways that denial can be helpful:

1 Denial can help us focus on getting things done even in the midst of an apocalypse by allowing us to put off processing difficult things until there is the time/need for it.

2 Denial can help us feel good, even when things are really, really bad.

3 Denial can help us maintain the best possible version of ourselves. That way, we can convince others that we're awesome and have a super-bright future so that they want to be our friends, mates, or associates.

4 Denial saves us from the costs of actually doing something about the problems we are facing and will face in the future.

5 Denial can get other people to fix problems for us before we have to deal with them ourselves.

6 Denial saves us from the trade-off of doing something about the problems around us. Meaning: If you spend time fixing problems, you can't do other things like hanging out with your kids, scrolling through your social media feed, or ignoring your kids while you scroll through your social media feed.

The positive ways that denial can serve us include both emotional in-the-moment reasons as well as deeper evolutionary reasons (ways that could contribute to our survival and reproduction). Evolution and behavior nerds like me call these different types of explanations "proximate and ultimate explanations" for behavior, respectively.

The proximate or immediate reason we like to stay in denial is that it allows us to avoid psychological pain. So denial can protect us both psychologically and practically from huge costs. Facing how bad things are requires a lot of replanning. Look at all the replanning the COVID-19 pandemic required. We had to give up things that we were looking forward to, find new ways of life that accommodated the virus, change our goals and approaches to achieving them, and grieve for many losses.

Denial can help us feel good even when things are bad, which explains, on a surface level, why we engage in it. But to explain why it exists on a deeper level, we have to consider its evolutionary function. It got others to solve problems for us, saved us from the costs of replanning, and helped us maintain a positive image of ourselves. But it comes with costs and at some point stops serving us. It is then when we have to face facts and detonate the denial bomb.

EXPLODING THE DENIAL BOMB

Life is crazy. We're all running from place to place, working, grinding, stressing, some of us trying to raise kids in a totally insane world. In this sense, there's no question that denial is useful for helping us deal with the more mundane tasks of life without being consumed by the fact that apocalypses are happening all around us. Some people see denial mainly as a defense mechanism that keeps us from feeling horrible feelings and freaking out, which is one way to look at it (this is called the proximate function of denial, to make us feel alright even when things aren't alright). But the fact is, we live in apocalyptic times. That means we have to explode the denial bomb and sit with the catastrophic risk that we face. And we have to do it right now so we can get our brains in the right place to handle present and future apocalypses.

Let's start by considering the immediate fallout you might be feeling after exploding your own denial bomb. Is it utter, mind-melting panic? Or more like a warm and terrifying radiation as obliterated denial begins to wash away? You might be asking yourself questions, such as:

- What absolutely has to get done in an apocalypse?

- What should we be doing when the risk of major catastrophes like wildfires, floods, and nuclear war is ever (or at least often) present?

- And of course, what should I do to secure the basics for myself, my friends and community, and others?

It might also help to acknowledge that perhaps some of your underlying, creeping anxiety comes from the fact that we really do own and carry a bunch of risk—meaning we know that we're on the hook for the consequences if shit hits the fan (as explained in Chapter 4). And, on some level, we probably know we're unprepared for those consequences as individuals and as a society.

WHAT REALLY NEEDS TO GET DONE IN THE APOCALYPSE?

Life can actually be simple in the apocalypse. To survive, you only need to take care of some basic stuff. Here's a fun mnemonic to help you remember the minimum you need to do, and in what order:

Sh Wa Fi Fo

Shelter
Water
Fire/Warmth
Food

In a crisis, first secure these things for yourself, those you care about, and your broader community. And then maybe ask yourself: What would be wrong with just prioritizing this stuff in general? Like instead of competing and consuming and accumulating, maybe we should focus on securing basic needs for ourselves, our families, our communities, and really everyone? It doesn't stop there. In this way, we can also think about securing these basic human needs for future generations. If we've all got ShWaFiFo, we've really got all we need to get through.

Rather than distracting ourselves from that apocalyptic stress (as much internet-based advice suggests), perhaps we should acknowledge that some of that stress and anxiety might be orienting us to pay attention to a bunch of risks. And that it might be pointing us in the general direction of a bunch of risks we don't necessarily recognize or realize that we own. And just maybe some of our generalized anxiety is coming from the fact that we want to better understand and manage those risks, not just individually but also collectively.

Making the Apocalypse Fun Again

Getting your brain to accept that the apocalypse isn't all fun and games isn't much fun itself. But you know what *is* apocalyptically fun? Mitigating your existential dread (and utter panic and apocalyptic stress plus feelings of dire helplessness) with a good ol' apocalypse party (see page 57).

Fun solves a lot of problems. It de-stresses us, revitalizes us, brings us together, and even opens a window for us to face the reality of how fucked up our world is without having to freak out about it. It can also help us push past the desire to look the other way and pretend the end of the world is not hurtling toward us as we sip our lattes and scroll our social media feeds. Fun can help us let go of the fear and avoidance that thoughts of the apocalypse can trigger. It can help us approach the apocalypse with curiosity, humor, and a mindset of possibility and adventure.

For example, in 2011, the Centers for Disease Control drastically increased people's engagement with all-hazards prepping by publishing "Preparedness 101: Zombie Apocalypse" instead of a more typically boring traditional disaster preparation guide. (Though they have since unfortunately retired the zombie apocalypse guide, partially because people were genuinely confused about whether there was an actual zombie apocalypse going on.) Similarly, the US military put together a training plan, CONOP 8888 (Google it!), which, according to its creators, "provided a very useful and effective training" for students, partially because it was "so ridiculous." They posted the entire plan online in the hopes that it would "provide inspiration for other personnel trying to teach topics that can be very boring."

But you don't necessarily need to invite zombies to your apocalypse prep party to make it a good time. There are plenty of ways to make the apocalypse fun again, from geeking out over apocalyptic fiction (see page 53) to indulging in gallows humor as a way to cultivate genuine curiosity about the world and the reality of the risk we're all facing.

> **As long as we are intimidated and afraid, we'll keep avoiding (and not preparing for) the inevitable.**

Storytelling, humor, curiosity, and the ability to throw a really good party are some of the most important tools we have for getting over our collective denial about the apocalypse. Making the apocalypse entertaining is also an important way to avoid the perils of denial and avoidance. As long as we are intimidated and afraid, we'll keep avoiding (and not preparing for) the inevitable. But by having a little fun with the fact that we are living in apocalyptic times, we'll be in a better psychological place to learn from the past, engage with the present, and survive the uncertain future before us. So let's get on to the fun part of this chapter, where we talk about all the enjoyable ways we can immerse ourselves in the apocalyptic reality in which we're living. And, as everyone knows, a great time always starts with a great acronym!

PLAY BETTER CHESS

When I was a kid, I hated chess. Probably because my younger brother was better at it than me. But lately I've been playing a lot of chess (mostly with my youngest, who is also better at it than me), and I've come to appreciate the game's elegance and emergent complexity from just a handful of simple rules. Chess is about the balance between staying safe and going out into the world (or in chess lingo, protecting versus developing your pieces). Chess is also fun when you understand this underlying

tension—something I didn't appreciate until I started taking chess seriously.

The idea of having fun with the apocalypse might be a little hard to swallow at first. Thanks to the recent pandemic, all of us are likely accustomed to being miserable a considerable amount of the time, even when we're not facing the red-hot heat of an active apocalypse. We're also trained to accept shitty things from the time we're tots, so we just kind of put up with having a life that is often painful, boring, or some combination of the two. I'm not saying we shouldn't work hard, just that we should work hard on things that we're actively deciding to do because they are important and, ideally, also at least kind of fun. We should reawaken that childlike part of us that is curious and likes amusement, and then work hard on something that feeds that inner child with some delightfully playful apocalyptic sustenance.

So let's play chess. Or, more accurately, let's play CHESS, my acronym for the five strategies that we can employ to make the apocalypse into something that we actually want to engage with, a way to find that balance between safety and actually getting yourself out there in the world. With CHESS, we make contemplating and preparing for the apocalypse a kind of game. But we're smart about it, thinking through various possibilities for how we might move forward (developing our collective pieces) and carefully considering and covering the vulnerabilities that open up as we make moves (protecting our pieces). With CHESS, we can approach complex and terrifying problems with flexibility, openness, and a readiness to learn and cooperate. Here's how it works:

Curiosity. We humans are fundamentally curious creatures. We can harness that curiosity to learn about the apocalyptic landscape we are facing and how to handle it (ideally with less doom-scrolling).

Humor. Even when things are bad—especially when things are bad—humor helps us find joy, connection, and stress relief. It can even help us look at problems differently and shift our efforts to be more effective.

Entertainment. We love to listen to music, look at amazing visual art, hear from hilarious comics, watch fun movies, and read engaging books. Being entertained opens us up to new ways of seeing the world and can make it easier to learn and remember.

Storytelling. When we tell stories, we bring our shared attention and imagination to those stories. With apocalyptic stories, this gives us a chance to have collective engagement with things that might otherwise be too scary for us to really want to spend a lot of time talking or thinking about.

Socializing. Having fun, throwing parties, performing, and sharing information during intense times is one of the ways that humans deal with collective threats. Also, the connections that we forge through these social events can form the basis of mutual aid relationships that can come in handy during real catastrophes.

Curiosity: Risking your life to learn things

So many horror movies have that scene where the protagonist opens the door because curiosity gets the better of them. Typically, this ends in some deep life-or-universe-threatening shit that makes for an exciting climax to what might otherwise be a barely-worth-watching film.

You might not be into B-movie horror, but maybe you like true crime podcasts or you're really into slowing down *a lot* as you pass car accidents or you love those safari parks where you can take glamour shots with big cats that could bite your head off. (Or possibly you're just the kind of person who would pick up a book about the apocalypse because it sounds like a fun read.) If so, you get that there is something fascinating about the morbid, the deadly, the dangerous. It turns out we are fundamentally curious about things that threaten us. So much so that we're even willing to risk our lives sometimes to learn more about the very things that can kill us, a phenomenon known as morbid curiosity.

To understand why we do something as bizarre as approaching an agent of our potential destruction, let's take a step back and look to the nonhuman animal world for insight. Lots of organisms engage in something called predator inspection, perhaps the most common form of morbid curiosity in nature.

Learning about threats can help you be more safe in the future.

For example, a gazelle approaches a lion to get a sense of its behavior and the level of threat it poses. If, for example, a lion is lounging around lazily, perhaps after just having had a big meal, it doesn't pose a threat. Which means the gazelle can safely forage near the lion without worrying about getting eaten.

Like the gazelle inspecting the lion, we also need to inspect threats so we can figure out what to be afraid of, what not to fear, and how much we can operate safely despite the risks. That horror movie scene where the protagonist decides to go look in the basement is the human version of predator inspection. Sure, it can get you killed—but it can also save you in the long term. Here's why: The benefits from gaining information about the nature of a threat can sometimes outweigh the risks of the threat itself.

Oddly, people in horror movies are a little like chess players; both need to balance two important goals: (1) keeping yourself safe from the threats and (2) knowing how much risk you can afford to take as you go about your life. If you don't explore the world at all and you just stay holed up in your den (or bunker), you're going to miss out on life. Sometimes you have to get up close and terrifyingly personal to figure out if something really is a threat, or if it's something you can safely ignore.

Humor: Dying for Laughs

One of the most effective ways of dealing with the kind of horrendous stress that swirls around death—whether it's the threat of your own death (not fun!) or seeing death in your day-to-day life (also not fun!)—is humor. Also called gallows humor or dark humor, it's used by doctors, firefighters, morticians, fighter pilots, and many others who have to deal with death, dismemberment, disease, and disaster on a regular basis. Making light of the most dire situations might seem insensitive (it often is) and counterproductive—because, shouldn't serious situations be taken seriously? Well, of course they should. But according to reports from people in these high-pressure professions, gallows humor is an important safety valve for the intense stress of dealing with so much life-threatening shit all the time. Laughing with other humans who are also dealing with extremely stressful, high-stakes, life-or-death situations makes it easier to deal with those situations.

Laughing temporarily increases your blood pressure and engages both your sympathetic and parasympathetic nervous systems, which can help to reset your nervous system if you've gotten deregulated by a shitload of stress.

But it's not only people in high-stress jobs who can benefit from finding humor in difficult situations. Studies have shown that laughing can have health benefits for everyone from teens to the elderly. Even people on their deathbeds seem to benefit from humor and laughter. Laughing temporarily increases your blood pressure and engages both your sympathetic and parasympathetic nervous systems, which can help reset your nervous system if you've gotten deregulated by a shitload of stress.

Lastly, finding the humor in tough situations can help you better maintain your composure rather than outwardly freaking out under stress. And it doesn't matter if that stress is coming from seeing death every day at your job or if you're simply worrying about a deathly future for the planet.

Entertainment: Chilling the Fuck out

Sometimes, we all need to just kick back and relax. It can be listening to music in the kitchen, a little Netflix and chill on your laptop, or going to Shakespeare in the Park for some old-school culture. When we're having a good time, we relax and become more open to new ideas, new people, and new possibilities for our lives.

Entertainment can also offer a certain kind of escapism, allowing us to get away from things in our lives we might want to avoid while helping us feel like our lives really aren't so bad. It can enable a change in perspective, allowing us to consider new possibilities in our jobs, families, and social lives we may never have before.

Entertainment can bring the apocalypse into our lives in a totally nonthreatening and a frankly really fun and compelling way. Imagining ourselves surviving really difficult shit can actually be super fun. So fun, in fact, that this style of entertainment has been dubbed "survival porn."

Have you ever fantasized about how you would be able to survive in a zombie apocalypse? How you'd survive on Mars à la Matt Damon in *The Martian*? Or derided the contestants on the survival reality show *Alone*, imagining how you'd succeed where they failed? If so, then you know all about survival porn. But why do we entertain ourselves with these survival fantasies? It's likely because we're practicing mentally for shit-hitting-the-fan scenarios. We're simulating in our heads and playing through different ways to beat the odds in an apocalypse. Practicing how to survive (even in your imagination) is probably good for survival. And it's quite likely that our ancestors who had the most fun engaging with the most pressing survival challenges spent time doing the same thing. And those fun-loving catastrophists were subsequently more likely to survive and pass along that penchant for imaginative survival porn to us.

Storytelling: Bringing our brains together

Storytelling, in the form of apocalyptic movies and other speculative fiction, can be a scary-not-scary way to start thinking about the apocalypse.

Storytelling can also be a way for us to draw our collective attention to apocalyptic scenarios. This imaginative engagement as a group is something that's almost impossible to accomplish with strategies built on fear, guilt, and other "traditional" ways of getting people to pay attention to things that threaten our collective survival. Consider for a minute how effective it is (or isn't) to look somebody in the eye, take them by the shoulders, and ask them why they aren't panicked about climate change.

Meme
A unit of information that can replicate itself by jumping from brain to brain, often mediated by technology such as social media platforms.

If curiosity, humor, and entertainment are individual-level strategies for dealing with the apocalypse, storytelling is a much larger tool. And we can use it to leverage our individual readiness to have a good time into a collective, culture-wide apocalypse engagement strategy. Storytelling does this by bringing us together around questions of our collective survival in ways that are fun and engaging. If the apocalyptic stories are entertaining, they more easily get into our brains, bypassing the cognitive immune systems of denial and avoidance that often make us reject the prospect of even considering world-altering/ending futures.

APOCALYPTIC FICTION

Think of apocalyptic fiction and storytelling as our collective version of morbid curiosity. I'm no expert on apocalyptic fiction, but my friend and colleague Ed Finn, who runs the Center for Science and the Imagination at ASU, is.

Here are his picks for apocalyptic fiction:

A Canticle for Leibowitz by Walter M. Miller Jr.
A monastery in the desert preserves the remaining scraps of human knowledge after nuclear Armageddon, keeping the match-flame of civilization alight across the millennia.

Oryx and Crake by Margaret Atwood
A satirical, lyrical, and occasionally hysterical tale about genetic engineering, hubris, and burning it all down that asks what aspects of our humanity are worth saving.

Parable of the Sower by Octavia E. Butler
California is beset by fires and crumbling infrastructure while an authoritarian runs for president on the slogan "Make America Great Again" in this prescient, terrifying coming-of-age story about the power of change.

Station 11 by Emily St. John Mandel
A global pandemic destroys civilization, leaving the survivors to piece together new definitions of community and identity through the fragmented ruins of the past.

Zone One by Colson Whitehead
This deadpan love song to the zombie genre imagines a New York region overwhelmed by mindless hordes as our protagonist navigates "accursed Connecticut" as they struggle to rebuild.

APOCALYPTIC CINEMA

Zombies

Zombie movies can operate on a number of different levels. There's certainly the predator inspection (see page 48) angle—zombies want to eat you. But these films can also be a way for us to explore the scary-as-fuck dynamics of infectious disease transmission and how things might play out in a crisis of that scale.

Here are my personal top five zombie movies:

1   *Train to Busan.* First, the movie is beautiful. Also, it's funny in a subtle and morbid kind of way. Mostly though, it's brilliant at showing the complexity of human social behavior in times of crisis. There is conflict, cooperation, selfish undermining, and heroically immense sacrifice— all of it set on a moving train.

2a *Zombieland.* So funny and also poignant. Bill Murray as a zombie is reason enough to watch it, but the bumbling and charming dynamics of the motley crew trying to survive together also make it super fun.

2b *Shaun of the Dead.* This one is tied for second place. These two make a great double feature for a zombie movie night. This is a hilarious movie about an unlikely hero that revolves around a superb British pub.

3   *Dawn of the Dead.* This 2004 film is the remake of the 1978 Romero classic about a group of people who take refuge in a shopping mall during a zombie apocalypse. So many reasons to love this movie, including a fabulous unironically ironic "shopping" montage. There are also some great Z-team dynamics and an unapologetic realism about some of the risk of, well, taking risks in a zombie apocalypse. No spoilers, but the ending of the movie offers a nice lesson about the value of sheltering in place.

4   *Anna and the Apocalypse.* A Christmas-themed musical zombie movie. Need I say more? Add this one to your holiday watch list now.

5   *Pontypool.* This is one of my absolute favorites and definitely the weirdest. It's a sort of radio play within a movie, and it's so wonderfully odd, in fact, that to tell you almost anything about it would spoil it.

Everything Else

Many apocalypse movies get the fun part of the apocalypse right: the industrial aesthetic of *Mad Max*, the pirate-y vibes of *Waterworld*, the sci-fi fun of humans in space, or the gruesome fun of zombie movies. They can also put us in a space where we collectively envision what it might be like to live in a different kind of future.

Here are a few favorites from me and my Z-team:

Mad Max: Fury Road. This film takes place in a grim, industrial, warlord-filled postapocalyptic world, but as a movie it's so damn fun. Great, fast-paced action, amazing cinematography, Cirque du Soleil stunts, and awesome characters.

Wall-E. Is the apocalypse actually all humans living on a space cruise liner, jetting around in reclining pods and ordering everything we need from a little screen while Earth is lifeless and stacked with garbage? Yeah, maybe! And that's the setup in this delightful, family-friendly apocalypse movie. One of my faves.

How It Ends (2021). What if you knew the end of the world was coming, but you didn't freak out about it? Instead, you decided to make things right with all the people in your life (while having brilliantly dry and matter-of-fact banter with everyone along the way)? That's the conceit of this lovely gem of an apocalypse movie. An "existential scavenger hunt for your soul," as one of the characters describes it.

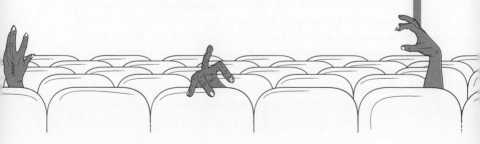

If scary stories are entertaining, we can engage with them without stress, which keeps us in information-gathering mode and insulates us from the dangers of being more mentally hijackable when we're under real-life stress (see page 51). There's even some evidence that storytelling contributes to higher levels of cooperation in small-scale societies, making it easier for people to work together effectively, which is pretty damn important if you're trying to deal with a host of looming existential threats in a coordinated way.

Stories allow us to think together about how we might then avoid the worst apocalyptic fates. Because the collective costs of not dealing with impending doom are . . . well . . . doom. But with stories we create spaces for ideas, theories, and data from multiple disciplines to come together in a kind of simulation, a collective imagination to envision alternative futures.

THE COGNITIVE IMMUNE SYSTEM

When new information comes into our brains, a whole sequence of events happens below our cognitive awareness to protect us from being manipulated. Just like our biological immune system is in place to protect ourselves from being hijacked by nasty microbes, our cognitive immune system is in place to protect us from being overtaken by nasty ideas, information, and attitudes (i.e., memes) that could have outsize influence on our behavior. Memes can infect our brains just like viruses can infect our bodies, occupying our mental bandwidth, utilizing us to propagate themselves, and interfering with our ability to accomplish goals. Our cognitive immune system sorts through all this new information, looking for incoming missives that might be there to pit us against our interests or otherwise harm us.

Socializing: Having an apocalypse party

In the bigger picture, having fun, throwing parties, performing, and sharing information during intense times is one of the ways that humans deal with collective threats. The Ik people of Uganda are a great example of this. Everyone in the village comes together to reenact raids from neighboring groups in an event filled with music, singing, and dance. Not only do they relive the tragedy and drama of the raids themselves, they also relive the experiences of helping each other. These events are serious parties, in every sense, and are an example of how we can do the same in the face of true existential risks.

The "psychology of arousal" is similarly useful in helping us understand the importance of entertainment during these trying times: It means that we will probably be in a better place to deal with the emotional challenges of grappling with our vulnerability to risks if we're in a positive social environment. There was a cool little study done in the 1970s where men who encountered a woman on a suspension bridge were significantly more likely to call her later than men who encountered the same woman on a solid wooden bridge. (The woman on the bridge asked the men to participate in what was a sham study, and then offered her phone number to the men if they had questions about the study. The real study was to look at whether they would be more likely to call if they met her on a scarier bridge.)

The creators of the study interpreted the results to suggest that the men in the experiment may have misattributed their fear of being on the bridge as attraction to the woman. Other researchers have argued that a better explanation for the results is that people actually find being around other people more rewarding when they are in adverse conditions. Regardless of how you interpret it, the study told us something very important about fear: That it is not a static, unpleasant emotion. Fear has the potential to morph from something unpleasant into something potentially enjoyable and motivating in the right social context.

We do know that people love to test their social survival abilities: People love Burning Man partly because it's hard to thrive in that environment and you need to cooperate and help each other to make it through. People will put themselves in challenging situations with others on purpose and then try to survive. But why? Part of it is that it's more enjoyable to survive when you're with others. After all, nobody wants to make it out alive alone. Having fun *together* is the true key to proceeding with grace and maybe even equanimity amid the apocalypse.

> Having fun *together* is the true key to proceeding with grace and maybe even equanimity amid the apocalypse.

The old European story of stone soup is a delicious little parable that drives this social point home. In the story, a few hungry travelers start a pot of water boiling to make "stone soup" after being denied food by the locals. The boiling pot attracts attention, and pretty soon a dozen townspeople have come by to inquire about the soup, and each adds a little something: an onion here, a carrot there, some rabbit, a bit of chicken. Everybody wants to put something in the pot if it means being part of the party. In the end, the entire town is involved and there's a great feast in which everyone takes part and the strangers are given beds in the finest houses in town as a thank-you. All because they turned nothing into something *together*.

When we're having a good time, making friends, or bonding with the friends we already have, contributing can feel really good. This helps us escape the trap of the social dilemma where everybody wants to avoid contributing. We can apply this same stone soup mentality to being prepared for disasters—if getting ready for the apocalypse is a party, then everybody's going to want an invitation. And they might just bring a leg of lamb or some root vegetables—or better yet, emergency blankets and extra batteries—to throw in the collective pot.

How to Manage Apocalyptic Stress

Apocalyptic stress is a term I coined to describe the unique kind of stress that comes from contemplating the end of the world and/or local apocalypses that seriously threaten you and your loved ones. "Apocalyptic" doesn't refer to the stress itself, but to what you're stressing about. Apocalyptic stress is akin to existential dread, but not quite as debilitating. It can be relieved by gathering information, assessing your vulnerabilities,

Apocalyptic Stress
Feelings of emotional strain and tension associated with contemplating large-scale catastrophes, crises, and creeping disasters.

starting on some basic preparations, and engaging with your community to better understand the broader challenges and opportunities. Also, if you can find others who share your brand of apocalyptic stress, then you can band together to do things and try to act on that stress in a positive way. Yay!

Managing apocalyptic stress starts by looking at stress more broadly not as an individual phenomenon, but as a collective one. Most approaches to stress management typically focus on the individual. For example, the mindfulness approach is really about how you personally manage your stress. I'm a big fan of mindfulness, especially as an alternative to mindlessness. Still, mindfulness, meditation, and all that goes along with it are but one part of managing stress.

If you're dealing with a demanding boss, needy kids, a partner who is driving you crazy, or you're just having a breakdown because Whole Foods is out of your favorite kombucha brand (never happened to me, I swear), then a little bit of mindfulness and some deep breathing can go a long way to getting you back on track. But, if you're dealing with deep existential dread because our world is already so fucked up and is only getting more fucked up by the day, then it's possible that meditating and clearing your chakras may not solve that.

Because these are stresses about the future we share—and that we share responsibility for—we need to deal with them together. But we still need to be able to manage ourselves and our individual stress levels, so we can be a part of that kick-ass collective. And that's why it's key to know what kind of stress you're dealing with and why: Are you stressed from a lack of exercise? Because someone (insert: boss, spouse, kids) has you fully occupied and you no longer have time for yourself? Because an agent of infection is messing with your nervous system (long COVID, anyone)? Or is it solely because our world is fucked up and getting more so all the time?

Luckily, there are techniques for identifying the kind of stress we're under and tools we can hone to keep that stress working for, not against, us. There are also various aspects of your stress response at the individual level that can be improved.

This will ensure you're at your best when you're contributing to the collective response that is meant to lessen the very things causing your stress in the first place. When it comes to apocalyptic stress, try to remember that you're not alone! Almost everyone is freaked out about the future, just like you.

STRESS REGULATION: PART ONE

When your body feels stress, both the everyday and apocalyptic kind, it leaps into action through a variety of processes designed to help you deal with that stress. Once your amygdala decides that there is something threatening in the world, it activates your sympathetic nervous system, which sends signals down either side of your spinal column into the very depths of your viscera where it taps out a neural Morse code to your adrenal glands. Your adrenals—two small, oddly shaped glands that sit atop your kidneys like funny little hats—then pump a bunch of bioactive factors into your blood to change your body into a crisis-ready machine. One of those factors is epinephrine, also known as adrenaline, which increases blood pressure, speeds your heart rate, and gets you ready for action.

Another substance that your adrenal glands make is the hormone cortisol. Cortisol is slower acting than epinephrine (in general, hormones tend to work slowly compared to neurotransmitters) but just as important. It mobilizes sugars in your body, getting them into the bloodstream where they can power your muscles and brain through whatever crisis you're facing. Your body is equipped to handle the stress, remember that.

STRESS REGULATION: PART TWO

Stress is a decidedly weird thing. Sometimes it helps us deal with challenges like running from a sharp-toothed predator or racing toward a vanishingly tight deadline. At other times it interferes with our lives, our work, and our ability to deal with the challenging reality we inhabit. And sometimes, it straight up paralyzes us so we can't do a fucking thing.

The mobilization that happens when your adrenals pump out epinephrine and cortisol is part of what is called the sympathetic

NERVOUS SYSTEM RESPONSE

Parasympathetic (chill) | Sympathetic (stress)

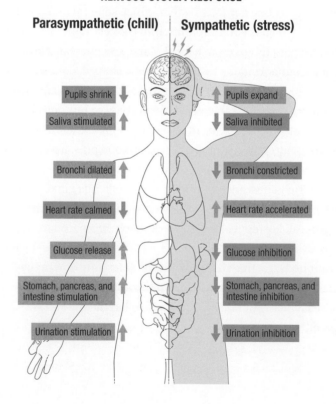

Pupils shrink ↓ | ↑ Pupils expand

Saliva stimulated ↑ | ↓ Saliva inhibited

Bronchi dilated ↑ | ↓ Bronchi constricted

Heart rate calmed ↓ | ↑ Heart rate accelerated

Glucose release ↑ | ↓ Glucose inhibition

Stomach, pancreas, and intestine stimulation | ↓ Stomach, pancreas, and intestine inhibition

Urination stimulation ↑ | ↓ Urination inhibition

nervous system response, as we just discussed. But there's a lot more biological machinery in our bodies that contributes to regulating our stress responses. In addition to the involvement of a bunch of hormones and neurotransmitters, we also have several nervous systems in addition to the sympathetic that contribute to us feeling stress and responding to that stress in a (hopefully) functional way.

The first cut is between the central nervous system (made up of your brain and spinal cord) and the autonomic nervous system, which is everything else. That "everything else" is then broken down into two different nervous systems (I know, why does it have to be so complicated?): The sympathetic nervous system is responsible for getting us all riled up when we need to jump into action, which we've talked about. The parasympathetic nervous system is what helps us calm down and go into rest and restoration mode when shit isn't hitting the fan. These two systems talk to each other, making sure we respond when we have to and we rest and rejuvenate when it's safe. But, like any relationship, if the communication ain't great, the whole thing can become super dysfunctional.

This means that your stress systems are complex and therefore inherently vulnerable to getting off track. They're teeming with positive and negative feedback loops that can get out of whack by way of chronic stress and trauma. The good news is that, if you're neurologically normal (whatever that means), you can hack your stress systems to keep your sympathetic and parasympathetic nervous systems functioning well and communicating effectively. Mindfulness is a hack into your parasympathetic; exercise is one for your sympathetic. These kinds of self-hacks help calibrate your system to "normal"

> Our sympathetic nervous system has undeniably evolved to help keep us safe, but ironically, we're also much more vulnerable when it's in charge. It's not concerned with nuance and there isn't much room to improvise when it's running the show.

inputs, leaving you less susceptible to getting hijacked (by someone or something trying to manipulate you) or just stuck in weird dysregulated neural-emotional loops.

A little bit of knowledge about how our stress systems work can help us understand not just why we get stressed, but also when our stress is functional and when it's not. And why our brains can completely short-circuit when they get overloaded with stress. Our sympathetic nervous system has undeniably evolved to help keep us safe, but ironically, we're also much more vulnerable when it's in charge. It's not concerned with nuance and there isn't much room to improvise when it's running the show. In a real apocalypse, it's essential to take in new information, process it, and respond wisely. And that's where goosiles come in.

Attack of the goosiles

Imagine you're sitting in a missile control room staring at one of those old-school green-on-black circular radar displays. The frontier of new information circles around from the middle, updating the image in a manner vaguely reminiscent of a modern loading icon. You're tasked with figuring out whether any of those weird blobby green shapes are missiles, and if you identify one you're pretty sure is a missile, you're supposed to initiate a sequence that will end in nuking the enemy and

HOW TO SET YOUR GOOSILE-DETECTION THRESHOLD

There's a basic equation that can help you set your threshold for detecting your own "missiles" in a world of goosiles.

$$\text{Threshold for detecting missile} = \frac{\text{Rate of goose encounters}}{\text{Rate of missile encounters}} \times \frac{\text{cost of nuclear attack on goose}}{\text{cost of not responding to missile}}$$

The more geese there are compared to missiles (the first part of the equation), the higher your threshold should be—meaning that you are less likely to respond to an ambiguous goosile. And the higher the costs are of launching a nuclear attack on a goose compared to the costs of not responding to a missile (the second part of the equation), the higher your threshold should also be. In other words, if there are a lot of geese around and the costs of launching a nuclear attack on a goose are really high (arguably both very true), then you should be really, really picky about what qualifies as a missile. It had better be really, *really* missile-y and not at all goose-y if you're going to call it a missile.

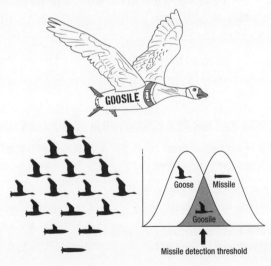

Missile detection threshold

killing millions of people. So, is that green blob on your radar screen a bit of weather? Or a high-flying goose? Or is it really a missile headed for your homeland?

Believe it or not, you and your nervous system(s) are constantly trying to solve problems like this. And like a radar operator trying to assess incoming threats on a messy green display, your nervous system is sorting through millions of signals coming in every second through your eyes and ears, looking for things that could do you harm. The problem is that the world is filled with ambiguity—the same green blobby shape on the radar screen could just as easily be a missile or a goose. In fact, they are goosiles: fundamentally ambiguous stimuli that might—or might not—be a threat.

Because some stimuli are fundamentally goosiles, there is no way to perfectly distinguish the geese from the missiles. This equates to an unavoidable trade-off: Either you correctly identify more missiles but also have more goose false-alarms, or you correctly reject more geese but miss some missiles.

There's relatively simple math attached to this principle, which goes by many names: Signal Detection Theory, the Smoke Detector Principle, Error Management Theory. The underlying

PRACTICAL TIPS FOR ROUNDING OUT YOUR INFORMATION ECOSYSTEM

1 Look at a potential threat from multiple perspectives.

2 Attend to all of your senses when assessing a threat.

3 Find as many dimensions of information as you can.

4 Talk to people who have different knowledge than you do.

5 Know when to stop gathering information; don't get stuck in a risk-assessment loop.

idea to all of them is the same: It often makes sense to tolerate some false alarms so you don't miss the real thing. But if the costs of false alarms are really high—like accidentally starting World War III by mis-categorizing a goosile—then it's really important to avoid those false alarms, even if it means a greater chance of failing to detect a missile.

In a world of goosiles, our nervous systems are doing their best to sort things into metaphorical missiles and geese. As with a military radar system, the costs of a miss can be high, but so can the costs of a false alarm. Constantly mobilizing your sympathetic nervous system to deal with threats not only takes bodily energy, it also leaves you more vulnerable to being exploited because your sympathetic nervous system is juiced to respond to incoming stimuli and is therefore blind to other factors. So is there some way to escape this seemingly inevitable trade-off between being too unresponsive to incoming missiles and overreacting to geese?

Thankfully, in real life, we don't rely only on a green blobby radar display to decide if something is a threat. We can gather information from many different sources and use that information in a way that helps us make better decisions. For example, if the green blobby thing is not just missile shaped but also moving at a missile-like speed and is hot as fuck because it's burning rocket fuel, then you can be pretty sure it's not a goose. On the other hand, if it's slow moving and lukewarm, then you can probably ignore it. The bottom line: A key part of managing stress is gathering information so you can figure out what you actually do—and don't—need to be stressed about.

STRESS-PLOITATION

The whole point of having a stress system is to help keep us safe from threats. But having a stress system can also make us more vulnerable to being exploited. As we learned earlier, when your sympathetic nervous system is mobilized, your body is suddenly ready to exert maximum effort and energy to respond. However, that readiness to respond can be exploited by other humans, and even microbes (see sidebar page 56).

When we're stressed, we often respond without thinking much about the demands put on us. If we don't have the mental bandwidth to process the broader context, we just pay attention to whatever is beeping at us the loudest (don't

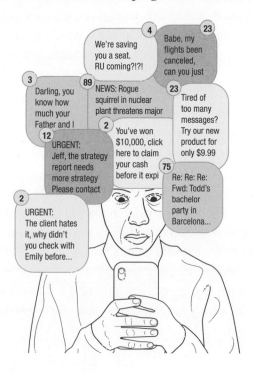

forget to turn off those notifications!). On top of that, our body mobilizes resources on all levels (including pumping glucose into our blood), so that we can quickly jump into action. When we're stressed, this means we're particularly vulnerable to being exploited by humans who want us to do things for them, institutions whose success is based on extracting value from us, or even agents of infection that can benefit by literally eating the sugar in our blood.

Stressing us out is an easy way to get us to shell out effort and energy, whether it's your entirely capable child whining for you to make them a snack, a microbe snacking on your excess blood sugar, or your employer feeding on your life force. It's no wonder we're all so stressed out all the time.

And because we can be exploited when we're under stress, this can give others a perverse incentive to stress us out. Which maybe explains why our modern world is filled with seemingly unending sources of stress. Because it's then easier to extract effort, labor, or even the sugar in our blood (if you're a microbe).

In the case of an apocalypse—large or small—you need to be wary of this vulnerability. And keeping yourself from being hijacked against your own interests is an important skill regardless of the apocalyptic status of the moment.

Here are some quick tips for how to avoid being hijacked by somebody or something that might not have your interests at heart (and how to know when to embrace it):

1 If you suddenly feel anxiety, fear, or a major shift of your attention after receiving new information from your boss, your spouse, or your online feed, ask yourself: Are these emotions and changes in my focus serving my interests, or

is some other entity benefiting at my expense from these changes in my state?

2 Cultivate relationships with humans and institutions that fundamentally share your interests and have a stake in your well-being, or at least have aligned interests with you in regard to a particular goal. For example, if you have friends who genuinely care about you, or if you work or volunteer for an organization, company, or institution whose mission you believe in, this makes it less likely you'll get hijacked against your own interests.

3 Take care of your body, which means protecting your sleep, eating well, getting exercise, resting when you feel ill, and being intentional about the substances you consume. When we're not taking care of ourselves, it can create a vicious cycle where we aren't at our best, making us more vulnerable to being hijacked, which depletes us further, making us even more vulnerable to being hijacked. Sleep deprivation, unhealthy eating, sedentary behavior, and substance abuse are all self-perpetuating cycles that fit this bill, and it's no coincidence they often go together.

4 Prioritize social relationships that help you manage stress and deal with the crazy times in which we live. Social support not only helps us deal with stress, it can actually help us manage a whole slew of risks we are facing now in many different ways (see page 170).

BEWARE THE RISK-ASSESSMENT LOOP

On some level, we're all more aware of the apocalyptic situation we're in than our ancestors ever could have been. We can track asteroids hurtling toward Earth, measure CO_2 in the atmosphere as it reaches dangerously high levels, and monitor seismic activity so we can sometimes be prepared for the huge earthquake or devastating tsunami.

Gathering information is essential when you're assessing a threat. But it can also be a vulnerability if you get stuck in information-gathering mode, never getting to the next steps of deciding if something is a threat, how much of a threat it is, or what you should do about it.

So how can we feel like we've gotten enough information to just get the fuck on with our lives and maybe even do something about our collective apocalyptic stress?

Here are some tips to prevent infinite doom-scrolling:

1 Put your phone in black-and-white mode to make it less enticing (this works so well it makes me not like my phone anymore).

2 Don't doom-scroll after a certain time of day.

3 Don't doom-scroll in bed.

4 Choose one apocalyptic topic per day or week, assess the risk, and make a plan of action before moving on to the next one.

Morbid curiosity is absolutely a good thing—to a point. It helps us get informed about threats and allows us to figure out how to live our lives even when it's scary outside (see page 48). But it only helps us if, at some point, we stop gathering morbid information, process it a bit, do what we can to deal with it, and get on with our lives.

THE THREE FS

You've probably heard of the three Fs, or some permutation of them: Fight, Flight, Freeze. When you get a jolt of stress, your body goes into a special kind of mode, preparing itself for what will hopefully be a functional response to the threats or opportunities before you. The first two Fs, fight and flight, are probably the most familiar—they both involve the activation of the sympathetic nervous system (see page 62). This activation is, on the one hand, a good thing because it allows us to respond quickly to threats. But our sympathetic nervous system can also be activated sometimes when there is no actual threat, and if our stress systems stay chronically activated, this can make us sick and/or miserable.

There is also the third F, freeze, which most likely evolved to make us invisible to predators that track movement and/or to trick nasty humans into thinking we were already dead. We freeze when we feel trapped, either because there's no way out, we don't know how to get out, or the best thing to do is to look like you don't exist. The freeze response happens when both the sympathetic and parasympathetic nervous systems are juiced at the same time, like you're pushing the gas (the sympathetic nervous system) and the brakes (the parasympathetic nervous system) simultaneously. You're frozen but also ready to jump into action as soon as the parasympathetic system lets up. This kind of active freezing is different from a passive kind of freezing that you might have heard of called learned helplessness.

Learned helplessness is what happens after repeated experiences with something bad that you can't control. Imagine: a rat in a cage that unpredictably gets a mild electric shock transmitted through the cage floor, or a human in a

HOW TO ESCAPE LEARNED HELPLESSNESS AROUND THE APOCALYPSE

Learned helplessness can be a trap. When bad things happen that you can't control, you can start to feel powerless to change them. And so many of the apocalyptic things that we hear about on a day-to-day basis feel like things we can't control. But there's a way out. Try these tips if you're feeling helpless and hopeless about the crazy world we are living in:

1 **Acknowledge and respect your feelings.** Yes, things are fucked up in the world. You're not crazy for feeling stressed, depressed, or even a little hopeless about it sometimes. Label those feelings and give them the space to be what they are. By labeling and acknowledging your feelings, you become aware of them in a way that makes it easier to use those feelings to solve problems rather than feeling stuck in them.

2 **Don't check out.** It might be tempting to throw your hands up in the air and say "fuck it," but in the end that's just going to make you feel more hopeless and helpless. Avoid the kind of all-or-nothing thinking that can lead you to feel like giving up. Even though the world is becoming increasingly apocalyptic, there are still lots of good things, and there are lots of things we can do to make it better!

3 **Stop doom-scrolling and do something.** Doom-scrolling feeds into feelings of learned helplessness by turning us into passive receptacles for all the crazy fucked-up shit happening around us. Sure, you could try yelling into the void by retweeting and posting and DMing, but that really won't do much besides potentially infecting the rest of your social network with feelings of helplessness. But if you choose just one small thing you can actually do, whether it's getting your preps together (see page 153), helping your neighbor with their preps, volunteering at a food pantry, or donating to a cause you believe in, you'll get yourself out of that negative cycle and start feeling less helpless.

4 **Build your real-life apocalypse-aware social network.** There are so many benefits to having an apocalypse-aware social network, including being able to share information, working together to manage risk, and having fun preparing for the aftermath of catastrophes (see page 82).

cubicle who gets randomly yelled at by a roving middle manager who makes inappropriately intense eye contact. After enough negative exposure in a situation over which you have no control, you can start to feel like, well, you have no control over your negative circumstances. Learned helplessness doesn't involve the same kind of readiness for action—that ability to jump into fight-or-flight mode—that the freeze response does. This learned helplessness response probably explains why so many of us tolerate being treated like shit at one point or another: If you're punished but you didn't do anything wrong, it can lead to feelings of helplessness that can make you more likely to stay in a shitty situation. How darkly ironic is that?

STRESS-Y EVOLUTIONARY MISMATCH

Stress wasn't actually so weird before the dawn of modern civilization. You might have heard the "zebras don't get ulcers" idea from Robert Sapolsky that we humans stress about all sorts of things that don't merit stress. But this is only half true. Surely many of the things we stress out about, such as traffic, fashion trends, and the trappings of wealth and "advanced" society, are ultimately not worth stressing over. But at the same time, evolution has endowed us with brains that really, really care about all sorts of things that would've made a difference to the survival and reproductive success of our ancestors. These include how we measure up to others and whether others like us or not, and, depending on who your friends are, that equation can involve things like fashion and finance (no judgment—some of my best friends are well-dressed economists and I am deeply committed to apocalypse-casual fashion). This means that sometimes we're stressed for reasons

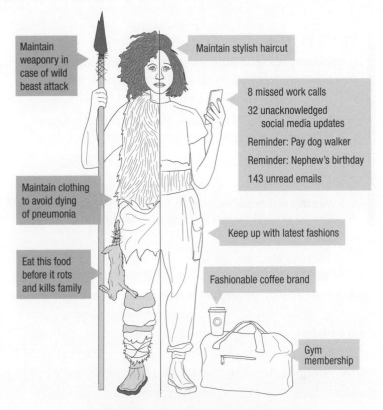

Maintain weaponry in case of wild beast attack

Maintain stylish haircut

8 missed work calls

32 unacknowledged social media updates

Reminder: Pay dog walker

Reminder: Nephew's birthday

143 unread emails

Maintain clothing to avoid dying of pneumonia

Keep up with latest fashions

Eat this food before it rots and kills family

Fashionable coffee brand

Gym membership

The challenges of today differ dramatically from those our ancestors faced, leading to evolutionary mismatch.

we don't need to be, but at other times our nervous systems are really just trying to do their best to help us survive, reproduce, and/or take care of our loved ones.

However, there are times when our stress system misfires because the situation we're in is evolutionarily novel. This is called evolutionary mismatch, meaning the world we're living in is so different from the environment we evolved in that our systems don't respond in a functional way.

ARE YOU SUFFERING FROM EVOLUTIONARY MISMATCH?

In evolutionary mismatch situations, you might be stressed because your body simply hasn't evolved to deal with stress beyond the circumstances that were common in our evolutionary history. Some examples are:

1 If you're not exercising (our ancestors had no choice but to do quite a bit of physical activity every day just to survive);

2 If you have low social support (our ancestors lived in tight-knit groups of kin);

3 If you are experiencing a lot of institutional stress (our ancestors didn't have bosses beholden to stockholders to exploit their workers).

The good news here (if you can call it good) is that our ancestors actually did experience apocalypses. They were a recurring feature during early human evolution, so we are, in a deep evolutionary sense, adapted for the apocalypse. But that means that our stress systems are more prepared to deal with a large-scale disaster than a boss with a Napoleon complex and penchant for put-downs. If you find yourself in the middle of a disaster with no preps, no knowledge, no social connections, and no idea of where your exits are, then your evolutionary-based apocalypse readiness isn't worth shit.

Our ability to deal with disasters is grounded in knowledge, preparation, and social embeddedness. And by realizing that we live in a world quite different from the one in which our apocalypse skills evolved, we can at least nudge ourselves in the direction of a lifestyle more similar to that of our ancestors. There are things we can do, like getting more exercise, prioritizing building and maintaining social relationships, and limiting stress that comes from interacting with institutions that are hijacking our energy and effort. Of course, it's not equally easy for all of us to do those things because of all sorts of structural inequalities and asymmetries of information. But knowledge is power, so learning about how and why we are vulnerable to getting hijacked is a great place to start.

And our social relationships are not just a source of comfort when things get tough—they can also be the difference between surviving or not in the apocalypse. Which just happens to be the topic of our next chapter!

HOW TO MAKE FRIENDS IN THE APOCALYPSE

03

If the zombie apocalypse happened tomorrow, who would you most want by your side? Take a minute and listen to that bestiary of zombies scratching at your door, moan-growling with visceral hunger. Who would you want standing next to you in the kitchen while you choose which cooking implement will be your best weapon against the horde? Maybe it's a childhood friend who has always had your back, a badass neighbor with even badder-ass survival skills, or a long-time coworker who's great in a crisis. Now think about *why* you would choose this person.

Is it because of your shared history? Their particular skills? That you trust each other? Is it because of their fun-loving-in-the-face-of-the-apocalypse attitude? Or all of the above?

I'm betting that the person you choose has a lot of the above, in any case. They're somebody you trust, who you can work with effectively, and who you love—or for whom you at least have deep affection. The truth of the apocalypse is that we need trust, cooperation, and even love to get through it and come out alive on the other side.

> There's no getting around the fact that humans need each other, especially in the apocalypse.

There's no getting around the fact that humans need each other, especially in the apocalypse. And because the apocalypse is already raging all around us, now is the time to make sure that you have your team together for the coming

QUICK TIPS FOR BUILDING YOUR Z-TEAM

1 Understand your risk.

2 Choose your friends carefully.

3 Find risk-pooling partners you can rely on.

4 Ask for help if you're genuinely in need.

5 Be there for your friends when they are in need.

6 Cultivate fitness interdependence.

7 Transform zero-sum situations into win-win situations.

8 Be alert to cons, cheats, and narcissists.

zombie invasion. (Note: We'll be using the zombie apocalypse as our general all-purpose apocalypse for the coming chapters.) As this chapter unfolds, we'll see how we can use knowledge from psychology, anthropology, game theory, and evolutionary biology to put together the baddest-ass survival team possible. We'll learn how having an apocalypse-ready team can make your life better, even if you're not dealing with an imminent crisis. Finally, we'll talk about how to capitalize on the benefits of cooperation without being exploited and how to maintain and cultivate a social network that helps you manage apocalyptic risks, zombie or otherwise.

Speaking of zombies, you might be wondering why . . . well . . . we're talking about zombies? Why a zombie apocalypse (ZA) versus the multitude of other possible apocalypses that could befall us? You might even be thinking, hey, Athena, the ZA isn't even a real apocalypse! I concede, on some level, that you're right—zombies of the slow-shambling, suburbs-terrorizing, brain-eating type aren't real. There's no way, thermodynamically speaking, that those kinds of zombies could energetically maintain themselves with the level of blood loss and the inevitable infection burden that would come from their gaping wounds and missing body parts. But there are a lot of other ways to think about the ZA: It can be a metaphor for a pandemic, a war, or even for a technopocalypse (where people are walking down the street so zombified by their smartphones that they're unaware of their surroundings—imagine that!).

Because the ZA is the best kind of all-purpose apocalypse for the morbidly curious crew, it's a convenient apocalypse to discuss when we're trying to talk about general apocalypse readiness. It's also more fun and less overwhelming than rattling off a long, varied list of things that might kill us all and then trying to imagine how we might get ready for *all the things*. And because—on some level—zombies aren't real, it's less scary to think about a ZA than the reality of the many hazards that we face. And even when it is scary, it's still fun!

Later, we'll talk about all-hazards prepping (see page 153), which means being ready for a lot of different possible emergency scenarios. The ZA turns out to be a great way of thinking about lots of dimensions of potential emergencies— disease transmission, the need to shelter in place during natural disasters, the breakdown of supply chains, war and civil conflict. Zombies and the ZA offer us an imaginative and useful way to engage with what is otherwise not so fun and get into that all-hazards prepping mode with a playful mindset.

Z-teams 101

Even if you've never thought about who you would have on your team during the ZA, it's likely you already have a few key Z-teamers, or at least a seed of a team that you can turn into a proper Z-team with the advice that follows.

One way to think about your Z-team is as your general apocalypse risk-management crew. Our relationships with those who can help us in times of need is at the heart of risk management for humans. This was true for our ancient ancestors and it's still true for all of us living today. Our ancestors survived because they had people they could turn to in a crisis, who were good risk-management partners, who were their Z-team.

Risk Pooling

When one or more individuals agree to take on one another's risk. With risk pooling, individuals can reduce the likelihood that they will face a catastrophic outcome because they are buffered by being able to get help from this network in the event of shocks or other unexpected negative events.

We need those risk-pooling relationships now more than ever, not just for the routine apocalypses (climate change, volcanic eruptions, the technopocalypse, epidemics and pandemics), but also for the non-apocalyptic moments where we just enjoy the company of people we trust and know will be there for us. These relationships are in fact essential foundations for us as a society to be able to deal with risks on any scale, especially those really large ones.

Many studies show that great social support improves our mental health and can make us more resilient to stress and depression, even in the absence of a catastrophe. Which brings us to one of the most exciting parts of all this Z-team building stuff: The very process of cultivating and assembling your team will make you feel better about your social world, give your day-to-day life more meaning, and help align your behaviors with your apocalypse-ready values. What's not to like?

Since having a solid Z-team is about doing a damn good job of managing risk, it's important to start with some self-reflection about what threats you face and what your relationship is to risk. You'll want to figure these things out so you can find Z-team members who share your general approach to risk, since that will make it easier to coordinate around all things risk-related. Start by asking yourself: What are your own risks? Your tolerance for risk? And how will you deal with all that risk? And in case you're thinking you don't really face risks or have to worry about bad shit happening, let's take a minute to talk about why you're not dead already.

WOW, YOU'RE NOT DEAD!

It's pretty amazing that you're still alive, given the infinitude of possible things that could have gone wrong from the time you got out of bed this morning to when you picked up this book. You didn't slip in the shower and crack your skull. You didn't get in a car accident on the way to Starbucks. And you didn't get flattened by errant construction materials while getting your steps in.

The point is that there are all sorts of risks out there we don't realize are ours to own. Building codes, Do Not Enter signs, traffic control systems and the like are all there to stop us from inadvertently creating more risk for ourselves. But there are also all sorts of "ambient" risks that we constantly face and don't necessarily recognize. Or that we wrongly assume someone else has managed for us.

This doesn't mean we need to freak out, stay home, and never hang anything heavy on our walls. But we do have to be aware of the risk landscape around us and know—to the extent possible—what risks are ours. And the risks around us can be those that we inadvertently create (like hanging deadly door art over your bed, as I once did), or they can be present in the natural world (like a flood), or be a combination (like the risk of having gas tanks in an area vulnerable to wildfires).

One of the reasons—perhaps the most important one—that you're alive is because you do a pretty good job managing the risks in your life. You're also likely part of a community system that, all in all, does a pretty good job of managing everyday risks alongside you. This isn't the case everywhere—some places don't invest as much in infrastructure as we do in the United States and Western societies in general. Some of this is because of differences in liability laws that affect how much investment in risk management makes sense for individuals, companies, and institutions to make. In countries where liability laws are weak or nonexistent, there's not much of an incentive to proactively manage risk. So being aware of how much risk management is (or isn't!) happening around you is important. It's also important to consider what your social risk-management strategies are: Do you rely on institutions and broader societal systems to manage risk for you? Or do you have a network of people with whom you coordinate and manage risk?

> Effectively managing risk together is one of the key things that makes a community. It is also something that we've been doing since our earliest days as hunter-gatherers.

Managing your risk starts with understanding it. Even more important is understanding risk together as a collective, because a unified understanding of our shared risk makes it possible to manage that risk more effectively. And effectively managing risk together is one of the key things that makes a community. It is also something that we've been doing since our earliest days as hunter-gatherers.

THE ANCIENT ART OF RISK MANAGEMENT

We humans manage risk socially and recover from disasters by helping one another. Without cooperation, our ancestors wouldn't have been able to cope with the challenges they faced. They might not have survived in the new and difficult ecological niches that they came to occupy as they migrated into wildly diverse habitats around the globe. It's fair to say that we modern humans don't stand much of a chance unless we're willing to help each other out.

And there are lessons in the past we can learn from. Small-scale societies today offer the best view of what life was like for our human ancestors. By looking to them, we can see what kinds of risk-management practices they use, especially how cooperation enables them to manage risk together. This is what my colleague Lee Cronk and I have done co-directing something called the Human Generosity Project, where, for more than a decade, we've studied cooperation and mutual aid in small-scale societies around the world. Our fieldwork has verified what we talked about a few sections back: that people report helping each other more, not less, when things get tough.

Our project started with the Maasai, a group of pastoralists (meaning they herd animals for a living, in their case mostly cattle) who live in and around the Great Rift Valley in Kenya and

Tanzania in East Africa. The Maasai have a relationship called osotua (literally translated as "umbilical cord"), a mutual aid system that helps them collectively manage risk. When a Maasai household is in need (say, a drought or disease killed many of their cattle), they can ask one of their osotua partners for help. And if that partner is able to help without going below what they themselves need, then they will help. This system leads to what's called a limited risk-pooling arrangement. It's limited because the obligation to help only kicks in if it does not put the giver at risk.

If osotua partners do end up helping each other, it's done with an open heart and no expectation of repayment. The only expectation is that they would be recipients of the same kind of help if they needed it in the future, which is very different from expecting to be paid back. It works out as more of a social insurance system than a loan.

Osotua, and the principles underlying it, can be hard for Westerners to wrap their minds around because the concept is so different from those of our market-driven, accounting-

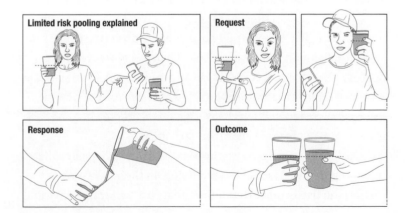

obsessed societies. When osotua partners help each other, they are not lending to each other and creating (even informal) debt. These osotua relationships are a social safety net, not to mention a great example of how we humans manage risk through social connections, in this case by sharing catastrophic risk through relationships of mutual aid.

This style of risk sharing is not just some quirk of Maasai culture; systems like theirs are common across human societies. We've seen them among the Hadza in Tanzania, some of the last remaining hunter-gatherers—and our best guess for how humans lived before agriculture—who share extra food they've foraged with those who return to camp hungry. Their need-based transfer system often follows what has been called an "eat-first, share-later" rule. This basically means the Hadza eat as they forage until they've satisfied their hunger, but often continue to forage, collecting food that they then bring back to camp and share with others. This style of sharing is called central place food sharing, because people come together in a central place (often around the fire) and share food.

SOMETIMES, IT DEPENDS ON THE ASK

One of the most interesting things I learned while studying ranchers in the American West was that their expectations about getting paid back depend on the situation—and specifically the challenge. When they helped a neighbor who encountered an unexpected, unpredictable challenge, those who helped didn't expect to be paid back. However, when it came to routine and predictable undertakings like branding and getting cattle to market, the ranchers expected that help to be reciprocated (every ranch has to do those things each year, after all). We also found the same pattern in a study we did online of people who live more urban lifestyles: They also did not expect to get paid back when needs came up unexpectedly.

HOW SMALL-SCALE SOCIETIES SHARE RISK

NAME LOCATION	SUBSISTENCE	RISKS & HAZARDS	INDIVIDUAL STRATEGIES	SOCIAL STRATEGIES
Maasai (Kenya/ Tanzania)	Pastoralism	Drought, disease, theft	Livelihood diversification, veterinary care, herd accumulation	Osotua relationships for risk pooling, risk retention, and group defense
Fijians (Yasawa Island)	Fishing and horticulture	Cyclones, droughts, illness, injury	Livelihood diversification, relocation, lifestyle changes	Sharing within households, kerekere need-based sharing norm, ritual exchange between clans and villages
Hadza (Tanzania)	Hunting and gathering	Variable hunting returns, wild animals, diseases, droughts, floods	Consumption of a wide range of wild foods, development of foraging skills over lifetime	Central place food sharing with those in need
Darhad (Mongolia)	Pastoralism	Severe winter storms	Cutting and storing hay, repairing livestock shelters, short-term migrations	Providing assistance to reduce risk, including building shelters and other preparations
American ranchers (Cochise County, AZ, and Hidalgo County, NM)	Commercial ranching augmented by small businesses and wage employment	Droughts, floods, injuries, illness	Livelihood diversification, herd accumulation, veterinary care, wells and stock tanks	Neighboring ethic (help given freely to those experiencing unexpected needs, chiefly from injuries and illnesses)

NAME LOCATION	SUBSISTENCE	RISKS & HAZARDS	INDIVIDUAL STRATEGIES	SOCIAL STRATEGIES
Ik (Uganda)	Horticulture, hunting, gathering, beekeeping	Drought, variable hunting returns, resource raiding by outsiders	Livelihood diversification	Widespread sharing (tomor) norm, with supernatural enforcement of sharing norm
Karimojong (Uganda)	Pastoralism and agriculture	Drought, disease, theft	Livelihood diversification, livestock movement, herd accumulation, agricultural intensification, food storage	Akoneo relationships; aid given to relatives, neighbors, acquaintances, and friends
Kijenge (Tanzania)	Casual labor	Chronic unemployment	Livelihood diversification	Kushirikiana sharing ethic

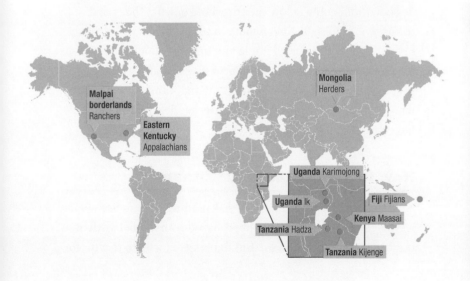

Need-based transfers also happen among Fijian fisher-horticulturalists who rely on their neighbors for help with day-to-day needs through a system called kerekere. Just like other need-based transfer systems, kerekere is based on the simple principle of not asking for help unless you're in need, and helping others if you are asked and able.

Modern-day cowboys in the American West, who deal with the challenges of unpredictable and often dangerous ranch life, help each other through a system they call neighboring. What we found through our fieldwork with ranchers in the Malpais region of southern Arizona and New Mexico is that they help each other in times of need, after a bad storm perhaps, if somebody is injured or sick. And unlike with predictable needs—like branding and shipping—they don't expect repayment for help.

Across all the different societies and methods in the Human Generosity Project, we have seen the same thing: People help each other in times of need (as long as they can do so without going below the threshold of what they need to survive), and they don't expect to get paid back when those needs arise from unpredictable and uncontrollable forces. Need-based helping is not just pervasive, it is also a strategy that leads to higher survival for individuals and communities who practice it, as I found in computer models that I made to look at this very question.

How to Jump-Start Your Z-team

Now that we've got the basics of risk pooling, we can use what we've learned to launch that need-based transfer network by building our dream Z-team. But figuring out who to recruit for your team and how to effectively build those relationships can be a challenge, starting with what red flags to look out for. So, let's begin with some tips for how to get started on the right foot with apocalypse-ready friendships.

APOCALYPSE FRIENDSHIP FAILS

Making friends for the apocalypse is a little different from making friends to go party with or just hang out with. Be sure to avoid these friendship fails as you build your Z-team:

1 Don't invite somebody onto your Z-team who is in denial about how fucked up the world is right now (see page 36).

2 Don't be afraid to ask for help if you are genuinely in need. These requests can initiate and help build risk-pooling relationships.

3 Never deny somebody who is in need if you can give without having much of a cost to yourself.

4 Don't look at prospective Z-team members as competitors; instead cultivate interdependence (see page 102).

CHOOSE YOUR (RISK-POOLING) PARTNERS WISELY

The first and most important thing in putting together your Z-team is to choose your partners wisely. In cooperation theory, partner choice is one of the most powerful ways to make cooperation more viable for a bunch of reasons, including: People have an incentive to be cooperative because it makes them a more desirable partner. It also means that, if you're in a situation where you're being exploited, you can choose to terminate that relationship and walk away (see page 100). So, being able to choose what relationships you want to be in is perhaps the best overall strategy for promoting cooperation.

A PREPPING EXPERT'S IDEAL Z-TEAM

I asked my friend and colleague Keith Tidball, a prepping expert and US National Guard commander, about who he'd want on his Z-team. He told me the key is to build a team that can cooperate well. He then broke down what he'd look for into three main categories: intangibles, hard skills, and soft skills.

Intangibles

1 Grit (i.e., not being a complainer)

2 No gloomy defeatist attitudes

3 No denial

4 Embrace the suck (the adversity) as an opportunity to thrive

5 Have the will to win/live

6 Stay focused on the current situation (don't dwell on the past)

Hard Skills

1 Pragmatic about food (not squeamish)

2 Conservative about using/sharing water

3 Know how to make a fire quickly, with minimal tools

4 Having a plan for dealing with shit—literally (i.e., good hygiene)

5 Basic bushcraft skills (using a compass, simple structure building, foraging, hunting)

6 Agility and good reflexes/athleticism

7 Know how to protect yourself, move, and communicate in challenging circumstances

Soft Skills

1 Good intuition

2 Mindfulness

3 Attunement and far-reaching sphere of attention

4 Communication skills, including literacy

5 Having a unique skill/talent/hobby that nobody else has

6 Be able to work as a team

7 Be able to be part of fluctuating/rotating leadership based on situation and needs

Embrace the suck.

Tidball also said that teams can cooperate well with these skills as long as there's not an ego hound in the mix, making it all about them all the time. If you've got one of those on your Z-team, I'm sorry. And if you're married to one of those, I'm even more sorry. I think you know what you need to do (see Walk-Away Strategy, page 100).

This is, of course, just one person's take on what makes a good Z-team. You might have different needs and preferences for your Z-team. Also, let's be clear here: Not everybody on your Z-team has to have every single skill—some people will be better at some things and worse at others. There are lots of ways to assemble a Z-team, and flexibility is certainly a good thing when it comes to getting the most out of your team!

So what kinds of partners do you want? What's most important to me might not be what's most important to you. But generally speaking, there are things that cut across most of our Z-team preferences. Most of us want people who genuinely care about us—and who care about the well-being of others—because they're going to be good team members. Most of us probably also want somebody with basic survival skills, like the ability to make a fire, some knowledge of the local ecology, and a certain kind of apocalypse-hardiness.

Once you've chosen who you want on your Z-team, the next step is getting them to actually join. Do you just ask them, "Hey, would you be on my zombie apocalypse team?" Sure, you could do that. But there are other ways, like starting small.

ASK FOR HELP

One easy way to form a relationship with a potential Z-team member is to ask them for help the next time you're genuinely in need. This is easier if somebody has already offered to help and you haven't yet taken them up on it. For example, rather than Instacarting when you're too contagious to go to the store, ask a prospective Z-team member if they can pick up groceries or stop at the farmer's market for you. If they come through, you'll have the beginnings of a need-based transfer relationship. If they offered to help, but ultimately didn't come through, then you'll have some valuable insight (read: cross them off your list and move on).

GIVE IF YOU ARE ASKED AND ABLE

Need-based transfer relationships can start with a request from one partner to another, followed by the fulfilling of that request. Among the Maasai, this is one of the main ways that these types of transfer relationships are established. So an easy way to start a new need-based transfer relationship is to simply help somebody who asks you for help (within reason, of course). In some situations, you might help regardless of whether you see the potential for a long-term need-based relationship—it's okay to just be a nice, giving person. In other situations, it pays to be a little careful about getting embroiled in helping somebody who might be trying to take advantage of you.

BE GENEROUS EVEN WHEN THE WORLD ISN'T FALLING APART

We humans have a fundamental desire to contribute to society and be a valuable part of our group. Our generous human nature is not only apparent in times of disaster—though this is often when it comes to the fore—but also in more "normal" times. This need to make the world around us better manifests in many ways. Most of us feel (or at least *felt* in our youths) the impulse to catalyze some type of change in the world to make things better. Many of us get more excited about projects if we're working on them with others, and feel more motivated to deliver if we know other people need things from us. And knowing that we're helping people leads to greater life satisfaction. For example, those who spend time volunteering experience immense psychological benefits, from reduced depression to greater feelings of social connectedness.

Famine

As much as we'd like to think that global famine is a risk of the past, the truth is it could happen again. In the 1800s, more than 120 million people died from famines that swept the globe—not from a single cause, but due to a perfect storm of problems.

In the early 1800s, China was hard hit and about 45 million died. Then, from 1850 to 1873, another 60 million died because of drought and famine during the Taiping Rebellion. Around that same time, the Irish Potato Famine claimed more than a million lives, while in the decades to follow almost half the population left the country.

And the risk of famine remains a threat today. In 2021, rain and floods destroyed 30 million acres of crops in China. In 2022, the UN World Food Programme issued a "red alert" saying that "conflict, COVID, the climate crisis, and rising costs combined in 2022 to create jeopardy for up to 828 million hungry people across the world." In some areas we are already "taking from the hungry to feed the starving." David Beasley,

executive director of the program, said in 2022 that more than 50 million people are knocking on famine's door, leading to a potential future famine that could bring about "hell on Earth."

Here are the circumstances that could lead to our demise from hunger:

CONFLICT

War and other conflicts can disrupt food production and transportation. Nearly half the world's hungry (across some forty nations) are currently dealing with civil unrest, conflicts, or war. In February 2022, when Russia sent troops into Ukraine, killing innocent people or forcing them from their homes, it caused serious disruption to the global supply of wheat, nearly one-quarter of which comes from "the breadbasket of Europe" (Ukraine and Russia).

COVID

Prior to Russia invading Ukraine in 2022, many countries were already struggling with disrupted supply chains and broad economic costs related to the COVID-19 pandemic. The World Bank estimated an additional 75 to 95 million people are living in extreme poverty in 2023, compared to pre-pandemic times. This vulnerability hits close to home as well. Since the start of the pandemic, some 12 million people have enrolled in the US federal government's food stamp program, with many relying on food banks for the first time.

CLIMATE

Extreme weather patterns around the world have created unprecedented disruptions and destruction that affect our ability to produce food. Increasing greenhouse gases and rising global warming are expected to intensify El Niño events, which in turn threaten the water supply—a major concern when it takes 1,000 tons of water to produce just 1 ton of grain. And if you think the United States might be spared, think again. NASA scientists predict a megadrought by 2050, severely disrupting agriculture in the US Southwest and central plains. And if you like beef, you might be in trouble because rising temperatures make cows less fertile.

COSTS

The prices for basic foods are soaring. Part of this is driven by rising costs of agricultural inputs. The cost of maize has been increasing by 90 percent year after year (yes, nearly doubling every year). Fertilizer and pesticide prices increased by 50 percent in just one year. Oil prices have been going up as well, and higher oil prices increase shipping costs. According to the United Nations' worst-case scenario, global food prices will rise by an additional 8.5 percent by 2027. World Food Programme director Beasley contends that we need $24 billion to stave off a worldwide famine.

BEWARE OF NEED-BASED TRANSFER CHEATING

Just like any cooperative system, need-based transfer systems are vulnerable to cheating. But the thing about cheating in need-based transfer systems is that it doesn't pay. In need-based systems, cheating by not giving if somebody asks you for help ultimately makes you more vulnerable by weakening your risk-pooling network.

Need-based transfer relationships like those practiced by the Maasai or Fijians can be a model for us as we cultivate friendships that can help us manage risk. Dr. Jessica Ayers and I have done some research to see what people look for and expect from friends. It turns out, having a friend who is there for you in times of need is always rated as one of the most important things (and, incidentally, your friend paying you back is rated as one of the least important).

You probably already have a bunch of need-based transfer relationships, even if you don't realize it. Do you have friends that you know will be there for you no matter what? And that if they help you out, they won't expect anything in return other than you doing the same for them? If so, you are already a hub of a need-based transfer network that exists in a market-driven world. And if you're living in an intentional community (otherwise known as a commune; a place where people voluntarily live and work together toward shared goals), or if you have figured out another strategy for opting out of the market economy, then need-based helping is probably pretty familiar to you already.

Need-based transfer systems are fundamentally based on relationships. This is both a strength and a huge challenge because, it turns out, relationships are difficult (in case you hadn't noticed). Building and maintaining them takes lots of time and energy. In realistic terms, they're hard, but they can be an inherently satisfying way to spend our time.

DON'T BE AFRAID OF COMMITMENT

How do we take our risk-pooling relationships to the next level? Across societies, these kinds of relationships involve deep, abiding commitments to each other's welfare. Commitment can allow us to reap the benefits of cooperation without as much risk of being cheated. But, ironically, commitment can also open us up to new vulnerabilities of being exploited.

If we look at small-scale societies like the Maasai, we see that their need-based transfer relationships (see page 86) are characterized by a great deal of commitment. (Once established, osotua relationships cannot be broken.) But that commitment starts with smaller interactions and grows over the course of a lifetime.

The dark side of commitment is that you can get trapped by it, and caught up in something that's not good for you. So, how do we build trust and learn enough about each other to commit without risking getting stuck in something exploitative?

There's an area of cooperation science called commitment theory that addresses this very issue. Here's the tl;dr:

1 Start with small acts of cooperation.

2 Ratchet up to higher levels as cooperation proves successful.

3 Don't just focus on cooperation; also consider if you are effective at coordinating together.

4 Have an exit strategy if things don't go as planned.

If you're building a Z-team of people with whom you want to weather the apocalypse, you can use these basic strategies to find and keep the right team. You don't need to fear helping your Z-team members if they're in need; just take it step-by-step, building trust with smaller acts before you have to deal with a ZA. And if a serious catastrophe hits before you have time for all that back-and-forth, don't worry. In times of catastrophe, people often go into a highly cooperative mode instinctually.

KNOW WHEN TO WALK AWAY

Because things don't always work out as we hope, it's important to reserve your right to leave a bad situation. I call this strategy "Walk Away," and it's exactly what it sounds like: you leave if your partner or team member doesn't cooperate. For example, say you're part of a friend group who are inconsiderate, or are in a relationship that's exploitative. The Walk Away strategy is to simply leave in those kinds of situations. It's kind of my pet: I came up with the Walk Away strategy when I was a hopelessly nerdy (but cool in my own way!) undergrad coding away in my dorm room. I programmed Walk Away to see how it did against other strategies in a standard two-person game theoretic framework for looking at cooperation called the Prisoner's Dilemma game (see page 110). Not only did the strategy do well in this simulated world, it actually

outperformed all the other strategies, including the retaliatory tit-for-tat strategy.

Walk Away is part of a broader category of strategies called partner choice strategies. Partner choice is a simple way to make cooperation more viable. It's also something we do all the time. It works because cooperators are more likely to interact with other cooperators instead of defectors.

As we'll see later in this chapter, many early game theory models showed that cooperation was a sucker's strategy. That, unless you were a cooperator with a vengeance like in the tit-for-tat strategy that punished past defections with defections, you'd end up on the losing end of things. Unlike those other game theory models, Walk Away is 100 percent cooperative and simply leaves defectors to absorb the cost of the bad interaction.

WHAT DO YOU REALLY NEED?

Take a minute and ask yourself: What is your threshold of what you need? In other words, what are the basics that you need to have to feel okay about your life? Will that change in the apocalypse? Because in an apocalypse we will be forced to reckon with the fact that we simply can't keep the amount of stuff most of us have now.

For need-based transfer systems to work, there has to be a common understanding among the people using them. And not just about the rules of need-based transfers—ask only if you're in need and give if you're asked and able—but also about what constitutes need. Which means we have to find need-based transfer partners (Z-team members) who share a similar threshold for what need is. In short, we have to agree about what's a necessity and what's a luxury.

Another good reason to consider simplifying your needs is that lowering your threshold for need could also make you a better candidate for someone else's Z-team. After all, would you want your Z-team composed of people with a higher or lower threshold for what they need? I'd definitely want someone with a lower threshold, because who wants a high-maintenance friend in the apocalypse? Not me. My threshold for what I consider necessities is pretty simple—it's the shelter, water, fire, food of the previous chapter (see page 42), including a place to rest my head that doesn't smell horrible. And a good hug every day, from somebody I trust. So what's yours?

Cultivate Feelings of Interdependence

Building a Z-team isn't just about who is on yours or the practicalities of how you're going to organize yourselves when the shit hits the fan. It's also about building emotional bonds that carry your Z-team forward through good times and bad. These emotional bonds are so important to our survival when things get tough that we've evolved to bond with people when we go through intense experiences together. Recognizing the reality of our interdependence with others, especially those on your Z-team, is an important part of getting into that emotional space where you can function most effectively.

WE'RE ALL IN IT TOGETHER
One way to start cultivating those feelings of interdependence on your Z-team is to recognize that our own survival is tied to our need for others to survive as well. This is the heart of

an evolutionary idea called fitness interdependence. People can become fitness interdependent because their fates are tied together in a variety of different ways—through anything that can affect their survival, well-being, and reproduction. This includes stuff like sharing descendants (i.e., children, grandchildren), engaging together in subsistence activities (like hunting, farming), depending on the same environment or group for access to resources, being engaged in the same intergroup conflict, and last but definitely not least, providing mutual support during times of need through risk pooling and

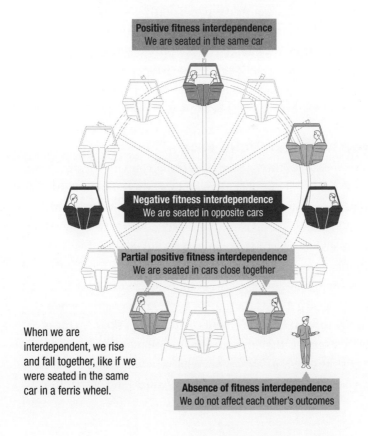

Positive fitness interdependence
We are seated in the same car

Negative fitness interdependence
We are seated in opposite cars

Partial positive fitness interdependence
We are seated in cars close together

When we are interdependent, we rise and fall together, like if we were seated in the same car in a ferris wheel.

Absence of fitness interdependence
We do not affect each other's outcomes

resource transfers. Meaning: Each of these areas is a place where you can enhance your interdependence with others if you invest in those activities and relationships.

The importance of having social relationships where we feel interdependent comes into clearest relief when things get tough. Throughout our evolutionary history, we humans have survived and thrived because of our relationships with others. This is the ultimate reason why we feel better when we are socially embedded. And when things are difficult and uncertain, this feeling of reassurance from being with people we can trust and depend on is particularly visceral.

A little investment in cultivating interdependence can go a long way toward developing the kinds of friendships that we should want to base our Z-team on—risk-pooling relationships where we intrinsically value each other, feel interdependent, and want to help each other because we genuinely care.

KNOW WHO'S GOT YOUR BACK

There are a lot of things to consider when putting together your ideal Z-team, but one of the most important is making sure the people on your team will be there for you during the darkest times. That means choosing people who are trustworthy, who care about your well-being, and who have the skills to come through when you need them.

Human relationships are complicated, but there are some general patterns that can be useful to recognize when it comes to what kinds of friends to look for in the ZA. One of those patterns is that humans generally have two modes for friendship: One is a debt-credit, what-are-you-going-to-do-for-me, you-scratch-my-back-I'll-scratch-yours kind of friendship.

The other is an I love-you-forever, be-there-for-you when-you-need-me, I-got-your-back kind of friendship.

Since the beginning of humankind, finding (and keeping) the right friends has been a crucial survival skill.

The reason that it feels so shitty to be dependent on people or systems that don't give a fuck about you is because being deeply and genuinely socially embedded is critical. And not just to our well-being, but also for our survival. Throughout our evolutionary history, people who didn't really care if those around them also cared about them were less likely to survive and successfully reproduce. Whereas people who freaked out if they suspected those around them didn't care about them did better (though freaking out on a consistent basis is definitely counterproductive for maintaining friendships).

> **Am I saying that evolution made us socially anxious and neurotic about whether or not other people like us? Yes, that's exactly what I'm saying.**

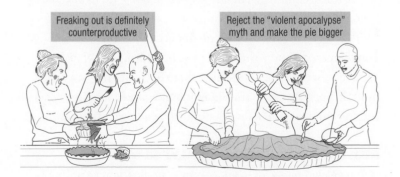

Freaking out is definitely counterproductive

Reject the "violent apocalypse" myth and make the pie bigger

Why fight over a small pie when you can work together to make the pie big enough for everyone?

Am I saying that evolution made us socially anxious and neurotic about whether or not other people like us? Yes, that's exactly what I'm saying. But there's more to it than just wanting people to like you—what we really want is for people to like us for who we are rather than just for what we can do for them. Being valued for who you are not only feels good, it also can ultimately make you more secure when things go south. So despite the cold-hearted allure of an economic analysis of friendship, valuing people for who they are rather than what they can do for you makes much more sense for the ZA.

The more you look at your social relationships in instrumental terms, the less likely they are to be what you really need for a ZA. What we need are people who value us intrinsically (and have a genuine stake in our well-being because we are interdependent), so that they will be there for us even when we have nothing specific to offer them. This kind of risk pooling is the heart of apocalypse friendships and Z-team builds.

If you are interdependent with somebody, their well-being becomes your well-being because you feel good when they feel good. So even if you and your prospective Z-team member don't have mad skills that make you both uniquely valuable to each other, you can still value them because they are *your* human, part of your team. Knowing that you value each other intrinsically can rachet up that mutual valuation further.

REJECT THE VIOLENT APOCALYPSE MYTH

If you've watched a lot of apocalyptic movies, you're probably all too familiar with the trope that our fellow humans will turn on us when things get bad. This can make for good TV,

THE 1906 SAN FRANCISCO EARTHQUAKE

After the 1906 earthquake in San Francisco, half of the city was homeless and the commercial district had literally gone up in flames. In the aftermath, people spontaneously created cooperative infrastructure, including setting up camps in parks to provide food and shelter for people who had lost their homes. This was accompanied by what author and historian Rebecca Solnit describes as a surprisingly joyous atmosphere. As one of the witnesses described it: "When the tents of the refugees, and the funny street kitchens, improvised from doors and shutters and pieces of roofing, overspread all the city, such merriment became an accepted thing. Everywhere, during those long moonlit evenings, one could hear the tinkle of guitars and mandolins, from among the tents." People helped each other when they saw need and had the ability to help. There was an almost complete suspension of market norms/transactions for several weeks, with stores giving away supplies, butchers distributing meat, plumbers working free of charge to repair broken infrastructure, and the trolley car companies letting people ride for free.

but the problem is that it perpetuates an idea that is not just untrue, but also could be damaging to our ability to cooperate together when things get bad. If we expect that everyone else will panic during the ZA, leaving us in an endgame nightmare (see page 117), then this anxiety and mistrust becomes a self-fulfilling prophecy.

The truth is: In times of disaster, humans are surprisingly cooperative and organized. If we look at how humans behaved during recent catastrophes, we see that more people step in to help and provide aid, and that chaos and taking advantage of others is the exception, not the rule. We saw it in New Orleans in the aftermath of Hurricane Katrina, with the spontaneous rise of camps that shared infrastructure and food. It happened in Florida, with people stringing extension cords across the street to share electricity with neighbors without power after

PANIC AT THE ELITE APOCALYPSE DISCO

Generally speaking, people are cooperative and kind. But if they're afraid, their reflexive responses may not be kind or cooperative because they're in a defensive mode.

Both trust and distrust can be self-fulfilling prophecies. A similar dynamic happens with panic. If people are worried that others will panic, then it can cause others to panic. In a disaster, we don't want to assume that everyone is going to panic, because then it's much more likely that everyone will actually lose their shit.

Panic can hijack our nervous systems, making it hard to think clearly about immediate threats and opportunities while neglecting important information of the broader context. Worse, collective panic sometimes infects vast numbers of people rapidly like a super-spreader virus in a low-ceilinged disco. But when it comes to actual catastrophes and people's responses to them, the reality is much more chill and friendly. That's not to say that there is no panic, selfishness, or bad behavior in times of crisis. But it rarely comes from the supposedly chaotic masses. In reality, it's not the masses who panic in crises but the elites. Disaster sociologists Caron Chess and Lee Clarke define this phenomenon of elite panic as a fearful distrust of the populace that prompts leaders to restrict information, over-concentrate resources, and use coercive methods to reassert authority in the face of temporary breakdowns in public order. This kind of response is problematic on many levels. It can increase dangers for disaster survivors or other vulnerable populations, create a self-fulfilling prophecy, and seed distrust in authority. The latter can then lead to resistance to authority— the very thing these leaders (and elites) fear most.

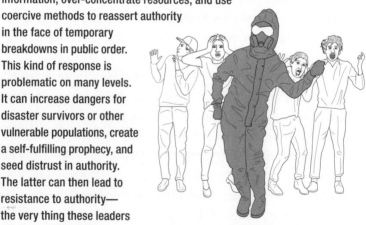

Keep calm and carry on (together!).

Hurricanes Andrew and Ian. And we also saw it during and after 9/11 and with the war in Ukraine, with outpourings of help and support from people around the world. After the wildfires in Los Angeles in 2018, many people returned to their neighborhoods to find no sign of their homes, but they did find help—and hope for humanity. As one victim of the Woolsey fire said, "Everywhere we turned, people were offering something— money, clothing, food, a place to rent. You really start to believe that people are inherently good."

All of this is not to say that everyone is always calm and kind in a crisis. Some people *do* panic, some *do* act like assholes. But the average, everyday person? That person is more likely than not to be an everyday hero when the moment calls for it.

Apocalypse Game Theory

Things are pretty complicated when it comes to cooperation in challenging times, but we've seen time and again how cooperation often works in practice when theories predict it won't. Now that you're (hopefully) skeptical of the idea that selfishness always wins, let's dive deeper into some basics of game theory that can be pretty fucking useful in the ZA, even if they're sometimes wrong.

Game theory is a super-useful tool for figuring out how to handle yourself in the ZA. By learning some of the basics of cooperation science plus the standard games within game theory, we can then apply them to the apocalypse and see how that changes things.

Game Theory
A framework for analyzing situations in which the outcomes for players are dependent on each other. It assumes that players are "rational actors," meaning that they're looking to maximize their payoffs.

PLAYERS, PAYOFFS, AND PRISONERS

The cold, clear heart of game theory is the idea that our outcomes are dependent. To know the payoff for a particular course of action, you have to consider not just your own choices but those of others, as well as things like incentives, values, etc., to ascertain what they're likely to do. This is why distrust can be a self-fulfilling prophecy, because if you think someone else is likely to screw you over you probably won't be willing to risk cooperating with them.

Game theory is unbelievably useful for reasoning through an almost infinite number of social, economic, and evolutionary scenarios. But most game theory was invented for dealing with situations where the behavior of other players looms large in determining what your payoff will be. When dealing with an environment that's highly variable, unpredictable, and uncontrollable (i.e., apocalyptic), some of the assumptions in traditional game theory break down.

Enter Apocalypse Game Theory, a term I coined to describe a subset of game theory that applies to catastrophes and other shocks. But before we get into the weeds, let's start with the basics.

The Prisoner's Dilemma

The Prisoner's Dilemma, perhaps the most iconic of game theory scenarios, is basically this: You and I have committed a crime together. The police have taken us both in for questioning. We can choose to both stay silent, in which case we both get a very short sentence. Or we can both betray each other, in which case we both get a medium-length sentence. Or only one of us can betray the other and get off with a clean record while leaving the other to endure a long sentence. This scenario is often represented as a two-player payoff matrix (see illustration).

Why is the Prisoner's Dilemma problematic? First, the majority of interactions between humans don't actually fit the framework of conflict of the Prisoner's Dilemma. Most of the time—and particularly in apocalyptic scenarios—we don't win

PRISONER'S DILEMMA IN PICTURES

In the Prisoner's Dilemma, there is a conflict between what's socially optimal and what is individually optimal. No matter what you choose, I do better if I betray you. But we each do better as a little two-person group if we both stay silent than if we both defect. But if I stay silent and you betray me, then I'm left with the worst outcome while you cash in on exploiting me. In other words, everyone wins if everyone cooperates, but there is a temptation to cheat and get a better outcome for yourself while leaving your partner in the lurch.

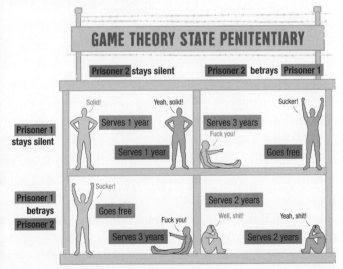

at the total expense of someone else. If we're dealing with life and death, where there's a possibility that we can help each other get through a shitty situation alive, then thinking in terms of the Prisoner's Dilemma could sabotage any chance of you and your partner surviving.

Stag Hunt

One of the most important game theory scenarios, arguably even more so than the Prisoner's Dilemma, is the lesser-known Stag Hunt. The Stag Hunt is quite simple. You have two options: You can go off on your own and hunt rabbits, getting only a little bit of food, or you can go hunt stag and have a chance at a feast. Stag have a much higher payoff than rabbits, so choosing to hunt them is the logical choice. But there's a catch: Nobody can successfully hunt stag on their own. It takes two to bring down one of those big boys. So, this means that your partner has to also choose to hunt stag for either of you to be successful in the hunt. Because if you're trying to hunt stag but your partner's head is in the bushes looking for rabbits, you'll come home empty-handed (while your partner will be eating rabbit stew).

The risk in the Stag Hunt comes from not knowing if you and your partner are on the same page. The risk is not that you might be exploited (as it is in the Prisoner's Dilemma), but that, in the absence of communication, you don't know if your partner will decide to also choose hunting stag. If you're worried that they won't go for stag, then it makes more sense for you to hunt rabbits too. But if you both opt for that low-risk, low-return option, you then both miss out on the possibility of a much bigger payoff that you could achieve together.

Luckily, solving the Stag Hunt is super easy. All you need to do is have a conversation with your partner. Either option has a reasonable payoff, and they are both what are called in game theory "coordination points." Meaning that, if you're both hunting stag or both hunting rabbits, neither of you has a temptation to do something different because you can't get ahead by changing your strategy (unless your partner changes their strategy, too). But of course, hunting stag together is the much better option (assuming you both choose it). In real life, and especially catastrophic and apocalyptic real life, our social worlds are much more Stag Hunt, much less Prisoner's Dilemma.

Sir Philip Sidney

The Sir Philip Sidney game is named after an English poet who was shot on the battlefield and, as he was dying, supposedly gave his water to another wounded soldier and said, "Thy necessity is yet greater than mine." Now, the inspiration for the name of this game doesn't exactly match the structure of the game that derived from it, since Sir Philip Sidney was dying anyway and gave the water he had because he assumed he was down for the count either way. But putting that unfortunate incongruity to the side: The basic idea behind this is that neither partner knows if they will be the needy one at any given time. The individual who has enough must decide whether or not they will help the other who does not have enough. If they don't help, then their partner dies and they are alone in the next round, facing the possibility that they will be needy and have no partner to help. If they do help, then both partners live to help each other another day. This is essentially a need-based transfer game.

Although this is a highly simplified game (as all game theory scenarios are), it makes it really clear that when our environments are volatile, our survival can be intimately tied to the behavior of others. If we don't know whether it's going to be smooth sailing or if we'll be up shit creek, it's best to share the challenges and the resources we have to get through them. Because even if it doesn't seem like it, ultimately we're all in the same jerry-rigged boat either way, dead or alive.

The Volunteer's Dilemma

Coordination is also important in what's called the Volunteer's Dilemma. As we learned earlier, denial can be a comforting way of dealing with the specter of an apocalypse (see page 39). And, in an ironic twist of evolutionary fate, we've been wired in such a way that we often take a lot of comfort in denying the risks we face. This almost certainly makes us collectively more likely to die than we would be if we faced those risks head-on (though, as we've seen, facing risks is costly, in and of itself).

OUTGROUPS AND ZOMBIES

There is a notion in a subset of prepper communities that during the apocalypse there will be "zombies" who will come to your house, bunker, or wherever you're hiding out, and vaguely threaten you but mostly take your stuff. Fearmongering is unfortunately central in some prepping communities—it helps sell guns, gear, and rations—and it can also fuel negative views about people who are different.

The problem is really when people see an "outgroup," or someone not part of their group, as a threat. And that those "other people" (or zombies) are going to come for your stuff when a disaster comes. That's when it gets ugly. And that's when the prepping strategies become aggressive—when fear drives them. When we worry about the zombies (people who want your stuff, who are not like you, who are another race, from a different background, etc.), fear kicks in and people end up getting second mortgages on their homes to stockpile weapons and ammo. This can also encourage zero-sum thinking, which poses every person in opposition to everyone else, redefining the world in terms of conflict, an often self-fulfilling prophecy.

GAME THEORY AND ASSEMBLING YOUR Z-TEAM

Game theory can help you see vulnerabilities that could compromise you when trying to build a kick-ass Z-team. Here are a few to consider:

1 **Don't get stuck in mistrust.** One of the important insights from game theory is that trust and mistrust can be self-fulfilling prophecies. But if we all understand that the game has changed for all of us in an apocalypse—and *how* the game has changed—it can make cooperation and mutual aid the better option. By showing that you trust your partner, it will help them trust you. (One small caveat: Be aware that somebody else showing trust can be a con strategy, so don't necessarily trust somebody right away just because they show immediate trust in you!)

2 **Beware of retaliation cycles.** Tit-for-tat mentality can destroy you and your community. So be careful: Punishment is not all it's cracked up to be. It can deprive everyone in a community of the benefits of having a long-term, positive interdependence with one another. It can often be better to reintegrate people into the community and help them build back their bonds. Many societies around the world use this approach, called restorative justice, which seeks to make the damage right rather than punishing the offender. If you're trying to build and manage an effective Z-team, restorative justice is likely a much better strategy than retaliative punishment.

3 **Some people are just assholes.** Unfortunately, exploiters can fuck things up for everyone else. People who are inept, uncaring, or focused on their own egos can end up doing things that make them feel good about themselves regardless of how it affects others, sinking an otherwise cooperative group. You need to watch out for leaders who exploit group members, hijacking them for their own ends. If you're in a partnership or group with an asshole, the best thing is usually to try to Walk Away (see page 100). If that's not an option, try to make things better before opting for punishment. Because, retaliation (see #2).

4 Don't get sucked into endgame mentality. Try not to let the end of the world get you thinking that tomorrow doesn't matter and that cooperation is pointless. Quite the opposite! We need each other even more when we're facing existential risks. Stay engaged and empowered, and embrace the uncertainty as a reason to cultivate that Z-team!

You don't want to be that person on the street corner prophesying the end of the world. Not just because it makes you look unhinged, but because being *the only one* spending time and energy trying to do something about a coming apocalypse puts you at a disadvantage relative to everyone else waiting for somebody else to do something about it. Plus, one person trying to do something about a pending catastrophe won't be able to do much on their own (which might explain why that person is on a street corner trying to convince anyone else that the end is near).

This situation is called a Volunteer's Dilemma. In this scenario, there is something that needs to get done (say, piling up sandbags to keep the neighborhood from flooding) and everyone has to decide if they're going to volunteer to help or sit on their asses and hope that enough other people will volunteer to get the job done. Basically, in these situations, everyone is screwed unless enough people volunteer and do something to deal with the problem.

I'm not going to lie to you—it's costly to face the apocalypse and change your mindset and lifestyle, especially if other people aren't willing to do the same. If you're then doing the work of preparing for the apocalypse and the people around you aren't, it's a lot of cost to you. It can be better to wait until everybody is on the same page. Problem is, if you wait too long, you're all fucked.

Endgame effects

Endgame effects are what happens when everyone knows that an iterated, or repeated, game is about to end. In Prisoner's Dilemma terms, it means that if both parties know when the game will end, then they know that the rational thing is to defect on that last round because there is no potential future benefit from maintaining cooperation. And if the logical thing is to defect on that last round, then it's only logical to defect on the round before that one, and so on. This ends up unraveling cooperation all the way back until you reach the starting moment.

MORE PEOPLE, MORE PROBLEMS

The more people you have, the more likely that some of them will be afraid and some will be narcissists with the potential to mess up everything for the rest of the group.

Problems can arise when we try to scale up human cooperation to a global level, which we need to do to deal with the catastrophic risks we face. But as groups get larger, cooperation tends to decrease (when all else remains equal). One reason is that it becomes harder for people to see the results of their efforts in large-scale outcomes as the groups get massive. Also, the incentives to cheat can get bigger as the pie grows: The more value a group creates, the more there is for an exploiter to exploit.

In large-scale societies, anonymity can also be an issue. It can be much easier for cheaters to go undetected because it's harder to find them in a big, impersonal society. In small-scale societies, generosity is embedded in the very social relationships that people cultivate and maintain. As societies get bigger, social relationships take a back seat to economic concerns and the pursuit of status. This makes it harder to maintain the kinds of safety nets that are a natural part of the social fabric in smaller societies.

DON'T WAIT FOR OTHERS TO HELP, GET IN THERE YOURSELF

If you see somebody in need, get in there and help if you can. Research shows that people are more likely to ignore someone in need if they see others doing the same. Don't fall into that trap—get in there!
Think you're not qualified to help? That could be true on some levels in complicated emergencies, but there's almost always something you can do to help. For example, take a car accident: Even if you have no first aid training, you could still be there to just comfort and reassure somebody while you wait for more qualified help to arrive. That is a huge thing to do for somebody who is suffering.

Facing the reality that there will be an end can sometimes lead to "end-of-the-world behavior." This kind of endgame effect can be a self-fulfilling prophecy of sorts, leading to catastrophes as people start to act like the end is near.

But here's the funny thing about endgame effects: They don't happen if you don't know when the actual end is going to come, even if you know it'll happen eventually. Which means that just a little uncertainty about the apocalypse can keep us cooperating, even in games like the Prisoner's Dilemma where the optimal individual thing can be to defect. So uncertainty about the end is good, in some ways.

There are other ways that uncertainty can be good in the apocalypse. In the Human Generosity Project, we've seen that people are much more likely to adopt a helping mindset when the disasters are unpredictable. This means that uncertainty about when a catastrophe is going to hit can actually be a good thing for our Z-teams sometimes. Uncertainty can put us in a mental place where we're more likely to help others in need without expecting anything in return, and where others are more likely to help us if we need it.

BECOME THE Z-TEAM MEMBER YOU SEEK

There is something really nice about being a person who is prepared for the unexpected. I experience a certain glee when I open up my car kit (a khaki duffel filled with basic motor safety and survival gear) to pull out my first aid kit, or super-handy baby wipes, or just-in-case work gloves because an unexpected situation has arisen. I might not be my dream Z-team member, but after a few years of work I can at least say I'm the kind of person I'd be reasonably satisfied to have on my own Z-team.

There are lots of reasons to become the Z-team member you seek. For one, it's great motivation to be prepared for unexpected events and catastrophes (see the next chapter

THE BENEFITS OF HELPING LOCALLY

How can you use your time, energy, and money to help others most effectively? A whole movement called Effective Altruism is dedicated to answering this question and helping people figure out how to be most effective at making a positive difference in the world. There are many ways to go about this goal, including making a bunch of money and giving it to the charities that most efficiently save lives, feed people, or whatever other goal you zero in on for your altruistic activities. But there are many benefits to helping locally, and many don't require bunches of money. Not only does helping within your community help you build your Z-team, it also can be a really efficient use of your time and energy (even your money, if you choose to donate) because that kind of local helping can happen with fewer intermediaries. It's also more rewarding to be able to see the positive effects that come from helping your local community. (Probably a nice little reward that evolution equipped us with for positive reinforcement when we're building our risk-pooling networks and social groups!)

for more on how to be prepared). For two, if you become the Z-team member you're seeking, you are probably cultivating some general apocalypse skills and readiness that other people would want on *their* Z-teams. For three, being apocalypse-popular is so much better than being high-school popular. Plus, if you are an awesome Z-team member yourself, then at least you know you'll have you to count on in case something goes wrong.

Be kind, be helpful, add value

One of the best ways to become the Z-team member that you (and many others) seek is to be kind, helpful, and someone who adds value to your community. Not sure what to do or where to start? Begin by figuring out what kinds of things you like to do to help others, and then start doing them. Think about what you're good at that could also add value to your community. In fact, if you want you could even make a Venn diagram of all the things you like to do to help others and all the things you're good at, and all the things that might be useful in the ZA. And then do the things that fit in that overlapping space. Doing these simple tasks can make you a valued member of your community, and the kind of Z-team member that others are going to want on their teams in the apocalypse.

HOW TO SURVIVE THE BIG ONE

04

You've made it more than halfway through a book about the apocalypse without the world ending. Congratulations!

It is no small feat to be part of a technologically advanced society that has yet to destroy itself.

But why *haven't* we destroyed ourselves yet, you may ask? Well, partly because humans are pretty resilient to catastrophes. We're also able to cooperate on vast scales, using complex information and flexible systems to do really cool things, including not dying. But keeping a civilization from destroying itself as it continually increases in scale and complexity? That's a surprisingly tall order.

Back in the day, a smarty-pants physicist named Enrico Fermi brought up a simultaneously inspiring and disturbing idea. He asked: Why haven't we found other life in the universe? Given the vastness of the cosmos and how long it has been in existence in evolutionary terms, why hasn't intelligent life emerged and made contact with us? Named after its originator, this conundrum became known as Fermi's Paradox. It can be summed up in the question that Fermi (essentially) first posed: Where the fuck is everybody else?

Another smart guy—a cosmologist named Carl Sagan—proposed a

> If you have technology powerful enough to propel life to other planets, it's likely powerful enough to destroy the intelligent life that created it.

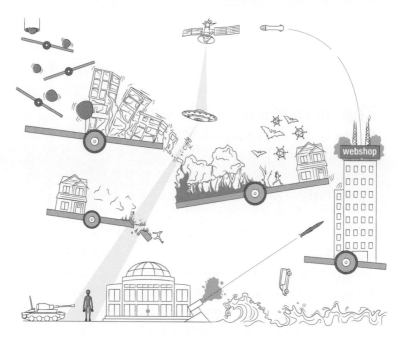

Holy clusterfuck: Disasters increase the likelihood of other disasters.

resolution to Fermi's Paradox: that intelligent, technologically advanced life tends to self-destruct. As technology advances and could allow intelligent life to explore the cosmos and communicate with other life in the galaxy, so does the capacity for (and risk of) accidentally (or intentionally) destroying everything in the process. Meaning: If you have technology powerful enough to propel life to other planets, it's likely powerful enough to destroy the intelligent life that created it.

So, in an intergalactic kind of way, it's amazing we're still here.

Long-term survival will surely involve continuing to grapple with the fact that we have the ability to destroy ourselves, be it with atomic bombs, lab-made viruses, rogue AI, climate change, or by becoming so utterly zombified by our devices that we lose our humanity. Some of these catastrophic risks have just sort of crept up on us as societies became more complex. Others arose as technologies quickly advanced and our scientific understanding of the world allowed us to do things no humans could do before (see: splitting atoms, creating artificial intelligence, and hacking into peoples' dopamine systems with tiny overlords that we willingly carry around at all times in our pockets). The scale of the catastrophes we face continues to increase as well. We're dealing with more people (than ever on Earth), longer timeframes (our actions today can affect future generations far, far into the future), and more complex and interconnected systems (from supply chains to the internet to our many complicated institutions) than ever before.

Clusterfuck Apocalypse
A disaster that increases the likelihood of other disasters, leading to multiple simultaneous and interdependent apocalypses.

So when we talk about how to survive "The Big One," we're talking about a modern clusterfuck apocalypse of massive scale and complexity.

In this chapter, we'll tackle the question of how we can keep existing as our societal capacity for self-destruction keeps escalating in both subtle and not-so-subtle ways. We'll look at what happens to all our awesome risk-management abilities when things get really complicated. Yes, we have a lot of amazing abilities to handle disasters, but the kinds of problems we face today are on a totally different scale than what our ancestors faced. Our problems now are wicked and super entangled: a pandemic apocalypse that triggers global supply-chain breakdowns, which leaves hospitals unable to provide masks for doctors, which only worsens the pandemic; runaway climate change that dries up our rivers, which leads to apocalyptic wildfires, which then destroy hundreds of thousands of acres of forest, further contributing to climate change; and so on. One catastrophe begets another, making it more likely that future apocalypses will be clusterfucks rather than solitary cataclysms. Scaling up our ability to deal with disasters is now more essential than ever.

The Big One(s)

Before we start prepping for The Big One, let's be clear about what it is: The Big One is an apocalypse of vast size and complexity that requires large-scale coordination to both understand it and survive. In simpler terms, The Big One is a movie-worthy apocalypse so wicked in structure and with so many moving parts that it's impossible to define in a way that allows a single person to wrap their mind around it. It's a clusterfuck: a bunch of apocalyptic scenarios that exacerbate one another, creating something new and unprecedented that we can't possibly anticipate. One way this could unfold: everyday creeping apocalypses mixing with natural disaster–type apocalypses—put 'em all together, and you get The Big One, a mixed bag of apocalypses on a massive scale. Downstream consequences will beget more downstream consequences until we're all so downstream we're struggling to keep our entire civilization from getting washed out to sea.

Can't wait to hear more? That's what I thought!

HOW TO PREPARE FOR AND RESPOND TO A NUCLEAR EVENT

1 Make sure you have your all-hazards prep game nailed, especially your shelter-in-place kit (see page 159).

2 In a nuclear event, get inside as quickly as possible and stay inside. Close all windows and doors and keep them closed.

3 If you were outside when the event occurred, remove your outer layer of clothing (after you are inside) and shower with soap to wash off any fallout from areas of your skin and hair that were exposed.

4 Don't eat anything from outside, only eat food from inside.

5 For fuck's sake, fight any post-nuclear FOMO and just stay inside. Turn on your handy-dandy hand-crank radio, play some cards, get out your ukelele, and chill.

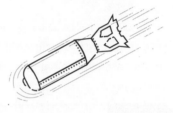

NUCLEAR EVENT

For many of us, The Big One immediately conjures the idea of a nuclear disaster. Since the Doomsday Clock was set up by Albert Einstein in the 1940s, the Bulletin of the Atomic Scientists' Science and Security Board has continually updated the clock based on their assessment of how close we are to the end. At present (mid-2023), according to the clock, it's 90 seconds to midnight—the closest it has ever been to the end of times.

Tom Nichols, an American writer, international affairs specialist, and retired professor at the US Naval War College, offers four likely scenarios for The Big One: mechanical accidents, human errors, a show of force, and reaction from a "sore loser" willing to destroy their own people to avenge an enemy.

Some say that the last time we were this close to nuclear war was during the Cuban Missile Crisis, a thirteen-day standoff during the Cold War between the USSR and the United States when the former threatened to put nuclear weapons aimed at the latter in Cuba in 1962. It was a defining moment during a period of geopolitical conflict between the USSR and the United States that began with the end of World War II and continued for decades until the dissolution of the USSR.

The Cuban Missile Crisis began when a bear was mistaken for an enemy intruder, almost launching the world into nuclear war. We came uncomfortably close to the end of the world during

---

How the World Could End

Nuclear War

How deadly would a nuclear attack be? A 2020 Princeton University simulation predicted that one tactical strike could result in the immediate deaths of 91.5 million people. This was based on a scenario of step-by-step escalation between the US-NATO and Russia in response to a hypothetical nuclear warning shot launched by Russia designed to halt US-NATO advances. And it wouldn't end there—worldwide famine would likely follow as massive amounts of soot would block sunlight, disrupt climate systems, and severely limit food production. This, in turn, would set off a clusterfuck of apocalyptic events that wouldn't end well.

A NUCLEAR GAME OF CHICKEN

Game theory started during the Cold War as the United States and the Soviet Union were locked in a dangerous game of potential mutual annihilation. It was a framework that allowed military strategists to analyze what the rational decisions would be for each party, given the likely payoffs of various outcomes. There are two game theory frameworks particularly relevant to nuclear strategy. The first is the iterated version (meaning that it is played over and over again) of the classic Prisoner's Dilemma game, where it is possible to retaliate against your partner's defection, as in a retaliatory nuclear strike. This retaliation-and-escalation dynamic leaves no room for stability and peace, especially when there is the possibility of errors and accidents that could set off a retaliatory cascade that could end catastrophically. The second is the game of Chicken, where both parties could gain a strategic advantage by committing to a decision (i.e., ripping out the metaphorical steering wheel so they can't swerve) that could be catastrophic if they actually did it, and neither party backs down so as not to appear "chicken" to the other. So, for example, with a very aggressive military strategy, one side threatens to drop bombs unless the other party backs down, and so does the other. If you think the other party will do it, it's in your best interest to back down. But if you can convince the other side you won't back down, then it's in their interests to back down. So, both parties have an incentive to intimidate the other into retreating, and can do that most effectively if they really are likely to follow through. Playing the game of Chicken this way only really makes sense if what you want out of the game is status and dominance. Otherwise it is, frankly, pretty stupid, for all chickens involved.

this Cold War era. Signal Detection Theory (remember our goosiles in Chapter 2?) was developed then, helping a generation of strategists apply reason to these crazy-ass times, when the costs of a false alarm could quite literally be the end of the world.

For a long time, mutually assured destruction (MAD) has—in theory—kept nuclear threats in check. The idea behind

MAD is that if both parties realize escalation will lead to utter annihilation of both their peoples, neither party will escalate. The problem with MAD is that it can also become a game of Chicken, where one party effectively commits to escalating if they don't get their way (akin to ripping out the steering wheel in the car-based version), forcing the other party into a very, very uncomfortable and unpredictable place.

We can only hope that MAD continues to prevail over the nuclear option. When Russia invaded Ukraine in February 2022, Vladimir Putin threatened nuclear force more than thirty-five times.

ALIEN INVASION

The threat of an alien invasion makes for great movies, TV, and tabloid fodder. But is alien life something we really need to worry about? The possibility of extraterrestrial life is all the talk these days with NASA acknowledging UAPs (unidentified aerial phenomena) and so many of us loving the wildly speculative opportunities and excellent movies about the prospect of alien contact, be it friendly, fierce, or farcical.

And we all want to know the same things: What would an alien arrival look like? Are aliens likely to be generous, technologically advanced beings that want to help us become more awesome? Or will they be evil, exploitative colonizers that want to take our resources, kill us, or worse? In short, what flavor of alien apocalypse are we looking at? And how are we to possibly prepare for their arrival? But really the question we should ask first is if there's even extraterrestrial life out there in the vast, vast universe. Because if there's likely not, why should we prepare for it?

Is there anybody out there?

I believe it's likely that life exists somewhere else in the universe. With 300 billion stars and 100 billion planets in our galaxy alone, and 22 trillion galaxies in our universe harboring who knows how many planets, it would be downright surprising if ours was the only planet harboring life. Of these sextillions of planets, a decent proportion of them have conditions that could support life. Our solar system alone has some 300 million planets that could support life as we know it. And many of them might be able to support life as we *don't* know it—organisms existing in more extreme conditions than us. Even here on Earth, extremophiles (organisms that live in extreme environments like super-hot underwater vents, dry-as-fuck deserts, and the ultra-low-oxygen stratosphere) routinely shatter biologists' notions of the conditions required for life.

And while I think the odds of alien life might be good, the goods might very well be odd. Life out there might not look like the wide-eyed, big-baby-headed humanoid type that has seemingly taken over our collective imagination. Interplanetary life might be more like clumps of bacteria taking a really, really long, unbelievably boring million-year journey across the galaxy, with their outer layer taking damage in a sort of intergalactic suspended animation from radiation and dying while their inner layers hang in there. More like an intergalactic microbial seed, complete with a protective shell (see following page).

Another reason to believe there are other forms of life out there is that all the building blocks of life (i.e., all the molecules that make up RNA and DNA) have been found in space and can be created there when meteors fly close to stars. These building blocks of life are in high-enough concentrations in comets that they could have seeded life on other planets (and maybe our own!).

Is extraterrestrial life a threat?

UAPs (the entities formerly known as UFOs) have been acknowledged as a real thing by the US government (in the sense that there is an annual report and a certain level of taking the whole "weird things in US airspace" thing seriously). This has fueled excitement and led to lots of talk about whether or not alien life is already here on Earth, or maybe hanging out in the stratosphere waiting to terrorize rural conservative folk and Sedona-loving alien enthusiasts alike. The not-so-exciting reality is that NASA's interest in UAPs has been largely motivated by security threats. They're concerned that these "sightings" might not be extraterrestrials, but rather instruments pioneered by Russia or China, for example.

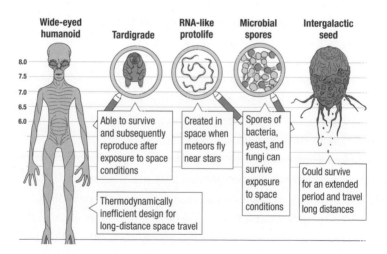

Wide-eyed humanoid — Tardigrade — RNA-like protolife — Microbial spores — Intergalactic seed

8.0
7.5
7.0
6.5
6.0

Able to survive and subsequently reproduce after exposure to space conditions

Created in space when meteors fly near stars

Spores of bacteria, yeast, and fungi can survive exposure to space conditions

Could survive for an extended period and travel long distances

Thermodynamically inefficient design for long-distance space travel

But if extraterrestrial life *did* come to our planet, would it be a threat? It's hard to say. We certainly have no data or lived experience about the relative friendliness of interplanetary species. However, if we believe that spacefaring alien life is anything like us, we might be in for a challenge. Historically, humans have been pretty damn nasty as we've spread around our own planet, exploiting and enslaving our own species and others. I hate to say it, but we can only hope that spacefaring aliens would not be anything like us when it comes to their attitudes toward colonization.

Some good news: It's likely that any alien life capable of making it to our planet would be sufficiently different from us. Either because they managed to not destroy themselves while possessing the technology to do so for a very long time—something we may or may not be able to manage—or because life from elsewhere that makes it here might not be technological at all but rather microbial life raining down from space. So maybe we stand a chance! Unless, of course, those microbial aliens infect us with something apocalyptic. So many exciting possibilities!

BIOLOGICAL WARFARE

Speaking of apocalyptic microbes, warfare using biological agents has a long history on our planet. In what might be the first documented case of biological warfare, Mongols tossed a bunch of plague-ridden corpses over the wall into the Crimean city of Caffa in 1346, to gain strategic advantage. Sadly, things have come a long way since the corpse-tossing days. Biological weapons can now be deployed quickly—and covertly—via aerosol sprays, explosives, or food or water contamination.

And worse, today's biological weapons are relatively easy and inexpensive to produce—for example, through new gene-editing technology like CRISPR (which stands for Clustered Regularly Interspaced Short Palindromic Repeats) that makes it scarily easy to change up the genomes of pathogens in ways that could potentially make them more deadly. You could buy your own mail-order CRISPR kits for just $130 in 2020. Not reassuring.

When we talk about biological warfare, we're referring to the use of microorganisms (including viruses, bacteria, and other infectious agents) to weaken or destabilize an enemy. In 2001, US military strategists conducted a war game called Dark Winter with a goal of identifying the national security, intergovernmental, and information challenges of a biological attack on the United States. Among the conclusions was that a smallpox attack on Oklahoma City could infect more than three million Americans within three months, killing north of a million people. Gulp.

When the United States ceased its biological weapons program in 1979, Russia did not, nor did it destroy existing reserves of anthrax, smallpox, Bubonic Plague, and other biological agents.

Many biological weapons that were developed decades ago continue to be a threat. When the United States ceased its biological weapons program in 1979, Russia did not, nor did it destroy existing reserves of anthrax, smallpox, Bubonic Plague, and other biological agents. Those highly toxic substances are stored on an island in the Aral Sea. Recently, Congress directed the US intelligence community to increase its biological intelligence activities to keep tabs on global threats, such as those stemming from biological warfare.

CLUSTERFUCK PANDEMICS

Pandemics are different from other apocalypses in that they fuel themselves. Because infectious diseases are, well, infectious, they can grow exponentially, impacting pretty much every system that we depend on in the process. I'm really just stating the obvious here, but it's worth spelling it out: In a pandemic, people get sick. This means they can't do their jobs and shouldn't go into their workplaces if it means potentially infecting others. We saw this play out in the early stages of the COVID-19 pandemic, which has arguably been a very mild pandemic by historical standards. Our supply chains were seriously disrupted, schools were closed, and our health-care systems were stretched to the max. In truth, it might've been a bit of a preview for what could happen in a more deadly pandemic, with everything taken up a few notches.

For perspective, consider this: Every year there's about a 1 percent chance of a flu that kills twice as many people as COVID-19 did in its first year. That's a frighteningly nontrivial chance that we'll be dealing with something *much worse* than COVID-19 in the near future. And we're definitely not ready.

Ideally COVID-19 offers a chance for us to learn and shore up our vulnerabilities for the next time around (and there will absolutely be a next time around). But, as the super-articulate science journalist Ed Yong has pointed out, we are not doing a great job of learning from previous mistakes and putting together policies that will help us deal better in future pandemics. "Pandemics are fundamentally collective problems," says Yong, "and they cannot be fought through policy that prioritizes individual action above all else." Most policy has been focused on individual behavior (e.g., getting vaccinated) rather than considering the broader social, political, and economic context in which pandemics spread, and the reverberating effects that pandemics can have on these systems.

Here's a list (adapted from Yong) of all the systems that are already overburdened that interact with, and worsen, pandemics:

1 Overstuffed prisons and understaffed nursing homes (hotbeds for transmission)

2 A chronically underfunded public health system (without the resources to manage risk ahead of time or respond to need as it arises)

3 Reliance on convoluted supply chains and a just-in-time economy (our supplies are currently delivered only right before they are needed, rather than having a buffer of supplies on hand)

4 A for-profit health-care system, whose workers were already burned out and underpaid (leaving us super vulnerable to a health-care worker shortage in the face of a fresh pandemic)

5 A decades-long project of unweaving social safety nets (leaving the most vulnerable even more vulnerable, which ultimately makes us all more vulnerable to pandemic spread)

6 A legacy of racism that had already left Black, Indigenous, and other historically oppressed communities disproportionately burdened with health problems (see above).

As Yong succinctly put it, "Future pandemics aren't hypothetical; they're inevitable and imminent." And we should be getting ahead of them with collective risk management and rethinking our infrastructure so that we'll be more resilient for the next time.

ARTIFICIAL INTELLIGENCE TAKEOVER

Do we need to be afraid of AI? Probably, but we aren't smart enough to know how afraid we should be, and whether we should be more afraid of AI itself or of the people building AI to achieve their ends. Sure, it's conceivable that we'll be able to leverage AI to improve human well-being and make the world a better place. But it's also pretty damn likely that AI will undermine humanity by design or by accident.

There's an undeniable irony to the way tech leaders talk about our AI future. For example, Elon Musk claimed that his humanoid robot Optimus is heralding a "future of abundance . . . where there is no poverty, where people can have whatever they want, in terms of products and services." But then he also warns that AI is "our biggest existential threat—potentially more dangerous than nukes." Putting aside the non-sequitur that a robot as expensive as a car could herald the end of poverty, Musk's contradictory statements capture our collective attitude toward AI: Is it our savior or is it the fifth horseman of the modern apocalypse?

> AI has advanced pretty far in the last few decades, but there are still lots of weird holes in its abilities.

Let's start by considering what we mean by "artificial intelligence." We humans have a rather narcissistic (surprise!)

way of looking at AI. It is often defined as any nonhuman system able to process information in a way that simulates human abilities. AI has advanced pretty far in the last few decades, but there are still lots of weird holes in its abilities. AI does a lot better than humans when it comes to solving problems that are very well defined—like how to win at chess or AlphaGo. But indefinitely multidimensional and open-ended problems (of which we have a lot these days) are much harder for AI. Also, lots of things that are super easy for us humans are really hard for AI, like detecting objects in a visual scene. That's why you're constantly being asked to prove you're not a robot online by selecting all pictures with stoplights or stop signs in them. What AI *can* do, like predict how proteins will fold, is actually really cool, in context. Because knowing how a protein folds can help researchers create new drugs to more effectively treat everything from cancer to COVID. Pretty great, huh?

That doesn't mean AI is all cancer-curing and chess-playing amazingness, though. There are lots of weird and deeply disturbing mistakes that AI continues to make as it's being developed. In a massive $62 million misstep, IBM's AI health-care diagnostic and treatment system advised physicians to give a cancer patient medicine that could have killed him. A facial recognition system designed by Amazon to identify criminals was put to the test with a series of photos of US Congress members. Not only did the software incorrectly identify some as criminals, but an inordinate number of those falsely identified were people of color.

Some good news, though. If you're concerned that AI will become self-aware and go all robot takeover on us, there are reasons why you can probably rest easy. First, we don't even know what consciousness is, and if self-awareness has anything to do with having the desire to take over the world. Second, evolution hasn't selected AI to have the same kind of appetite for resources and power that we humans (and many other species) do. We're probably worried about AI getting power hungry and taking over because we evolved to be wary of other human groups that at times wanted to kill us and take our territory. Finally, it's pretty hard to make a robot that can reproduce, repair itself, and do all the other things necessary to make an AI-powered robot takeover a viable thing.

If AI *does* destroy us, it's likely to be an accident or the unintended result of humans programming AI to do their bidding. Which makes me feel much better about the whole thing, really. Because if AI destroys us, at least it's most likely that it didn't *mean* to.

WHY EASY THINGS ARE HARD FOR AI

Here's Moravec's Paradox: Hard problems (reasoning) are easy for AI, but easy problems (perception, motor abilities) are not.

Why? Evolution by natural selection has had a *long* time to program us to sense our worlds and move around in them, but comparatively much less time to shape our reasoning abilities. Hans Moravec himself proposed the resolution to his own paradox:

- Skills that have been under natural selection for a long time should be harder to reverse engineer.

- Skills that are unconscious and feel effortless are some of our oldest skills.

- Therefore, things that feel easy should be harder to reverse engineer, and things that feel hard should be easier to reverse engineer.

THE SMARTPHONE APOCALYPSE

What would an AI apocalypse look like? Here's a scenario: Evil robots are taking over the world, killing and enslaving humans who are powerless in the grips of monstrous machines. This scene may not be far from the truth, but with a flipped script. Maybe *we're* the ones wrapping our hands around the monstrous computational machines that are enslaving *us* through the grip they have on our psychological reward systems?

Welcome to the era of the smartphone zombie. Americans check their mobile phones an average of 344 times per day, with about 3 hours total smartphone screen time. My screen time usage says my average right now is 3 hours and 39 minutes per day. That is a huge portion of my waking hours that I'm glued to this little screen. And an uncomfortable proportion of that time I spend on social media that feeds me a constant stream of information that I have no way of knowing where it comes from, if it's verified, or even fact-checked.

The smartphone apocalypse is already upon us. But are smartphones actually weapons of destruction or just a massive distraction? So much depends on who holds the power over them. Software giants and information purveyors (you know who I'm talking about) have a huge amount of influence and power over what gets delivered to our phones. This is a direct result of having so much information about our preferences and behavior based on how we interact with our smartphones and computers. "Everything [Facebook] knows about me can be used to persuade me toward a future goal," technology ethicist Tristan Harris pointed out. "And it's very powerful; it knows exactly what would persuade me, because it has persuaded me in the past."

All of this is happening because our brains are more vulnerable than we think. We can be easily hacked through simple behavioral reinforcement, a strategy that manifests in the many algorithms that operate under the sleek surfaces of our social media platforms. These platforms can exert control over your brain, distracting you with thoughts of picking up your phone to see who liked your posts even when you have your smartphone out of sight.

And the economic model for many companies involved in online spaces is of course selling our attention in some form. They attempt to influence what we buy, how we vote, and even how we post on the very platforms that are manipulating us, cultivating us as (unpaid) content creators, producing posts, tweets, and TikToks that ultimately allow those platforms to better manipulate our friends and followers who may want to see our information.

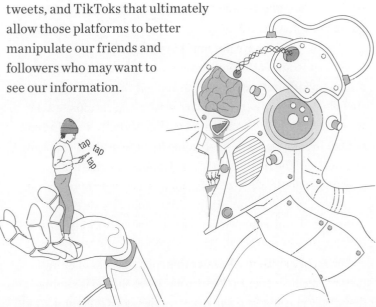

It's a brilliant, if sinister, business model. And some people are worried (myself included) that it could deeply erode our autonomy as individuals and our abilities to effectively manage conflict and solve problems collectively. (But hold up while I check my IG to see who liked my post about open mic last night . . .)

THE CLIMATE APOCALYPSE

There's no question that we're turning up the heat on this planet. From climate change turning our oceans into a rotting bouillabaisse of shellfish to death via unevaporated sweat to catastrophic technical fires caused by humans, there's a lot of world-burning happening. So let's muster up that morbid curiosity and take a closer look at the increasingly smoking conflagration we call Earth.

For a long time, we humans have known that we have the power to affect the environment and the climate through our behaviors and practices. The ancient Greeks realized that chopping down trees and irrigating deserts affected the weather. Today, a collective realization is finally dawning on us that the things we've been doing to our world are changing the weather, the temperature, the frequency of natural disasters, and the general likelihood of a climate apocalypse.

If you're looking for a proverbial canary in the coal mine, you'll find a menagerie of creatures whose existence is being threatened by the havoc we've wrought. We're on the brink of a sixth mass extinction, one that's happening faster than any other in the history of Earth, and it's going down on a massive scale all over the planet. In 2019 and 2020, Australian bushfires killed or displaced nearly three billion animals, primarily birds, frogs, and reptiles. In July 2021, a heat dome in British Columbia cooked more than a billion marine organisms alive, turning the shores of Canada into a coastal cataclysm for mussels, rockfish, and oysters unable to survive the heat. Along with a coastline littered with rotting crustaceans, the heat dome also killed nearly five hundred people.

And climate change is not just about sharp rises in heat events—it's a clusterfuck apocalypse (see page 125) that's a veritable variety pack of cascading effects, including extreme weather events, pandemics, rising sea levels, decreasing biodiversity, and economic inequality. Intolerable heat, wind, and rain can also encourage mass migrations. Economic inequality can lead to political unrest and war as people fight for increasingly scarce food, fuel, and water.

So have we passed the point of no return? Some scientists think so. But that doesn't mean we should just say "fuck it" and let the oceans boil. The more we do to mitigate climate change, the less bad things will be in the future. Climate change is one of our bigger apocalyptic realities, no question, but things could always be *more* apocalyptic. The very least we can do is try to prevent a complete lobster boil of a future for our oceans and planet.

WetBulb death

When you perspire, sweat evaporates, cooling your body. But if it's too humid, the sweat on your skin can't evaporate and your body cannot cool itself. If that happens, not only will you be unbearably hot (and not in the desirable kind of way), but eventually you'll get so hot that you'll just straight up die.

Our bodies need to maintain a temperature of about 98.6 degrees Fahrenheit for our organs to function, our cells to operate, and the proteins in our tissues to fold properly. When it's extremely humid and there's little wind or shade, it can be impossible to keep your body at a safe temperature. This is where "WetBulb" temperature comes in. WetBulb temperature is the reading you get if you wrap a wet cloth around a thermometer. The wet cloth simulates the potential cooling effect you can get from evaporation if you're a human sweating. If it's dry out, the wet cloth cools down as a result of evaporative cooling, giving a lower reading. If the humidity is very high, approaching 100 percent, 90°F can feel like 130°F. And just a little hotter than that and you're literally dead meat.

Even significantly lower WetBulb temperatures can be deadly. Some 50,000 people died during a 2003 European heat wave when WetBulb temperatures barely reached 79°F (yeah, only 79°F, or 26° in Celsius—this ain't no typo). In 1995, a heat wave in Chicago reached WetBulb temperatures of 85°F, resulting in about 700 deaths. Incidents of dangerous WetBulb temperatures have doubled since 1979. Physicist and philosopher Tim Anderson calls WetBulb temperatures "the scariest part of climate change you've never heard of."

Who started the fire?

Ninety-six percent of all wildfires in the United States are started by humans, according to the National Interagency Fire Center. These are often the result of things like campfires left unattended, the burning of debris, equipment use and malfunction, negligently discarded cigarettes, and intentional acts of arson. And while there's plenty of blame to go around, the important questions revolve around the extent of the threats, what we can do to avoid them, and just how likely we are to immolate ourselves if we don't address them.

> With the world getting hotter and drier, rendering more and more vegetation into tinder, with rainfall decreasing, and people increasingly leaving cities for wilderness locations, the chance of striking a match that turns into an inferno is high.

To clarify, there are a variety of different kinds of fires: wildfires (which burn natural materials), technical fires (which are fueled by human-made stuff like tanks of gas), and fires that are a combination of both. We tend to think less about technical fires, but they're a serious problem and include a wide variety of sometimes fuzzy causes, such as electrical fires, home explosions, weaknesses in a built environment, and of course, pyrotechnics at gender reveal parties. All these causes of fires are increasingly serious threats; as Jennifer Balch, director of the University of Colorado Boulder's Earth Lab, points out, "Climate change is making our fields, forests and grasslands drier and hotter for longer periods, creating a greater window of opportunity for human-related ignitions to start wildfires."

With the world getting hotter and drier, rendering more and more vegetation into tinder, with rainfall decreasing, and people increasingly leaving cities for wilderness locations, the chance of striking a match that turns into an inferno is high. And the aforementioned combination of wild and technical fires can be especially deadly.

One of many examples of this is the 2018 Mati fire in Greece. The blaze left 104 people dead—the youngest was six months, the oldest 93. Another 250 were injured, with 15 of them dying after being hospitalized. Many pets and wild animals perished or were injured in the fire. Thousands of vehicles, 4,000 homes, and 40,000 pine and olive trees were burned. When officials closed off roads, some 400 people, in an effort to stay safe, waded deep into the Aegean Sea—many carrying babies, many unable to swim.

"Armageddon" was the front-page headline in the daily newspaper. Officials declared a three-day period of national mourning. This fire was a combination of wildfire and technical fire, as the burn spread from the trees and grasses to highly flammable materials like gas and fuel tanks. I visited Mati many times in 2022 and 2023. I walked the streets and harbor area where the fire had terrorized the community. I talked with people about their experiences. The scene they described is almost unimaginable, with fire literally falling from the sky as the wind came over the mountains and created a giant blowtorch effect over the streets of Mati. Apocalyptic hellscape doesn't do it justice.

A smaller-scale technical fire tragedy happened with the detonation of a gender-reveal smoke bomb that ignited dry brush near El Dorado Ranch on a 103-degree September day in 2020. It burned 23,000 acres and claimed the life of a firefighter. The parents were charged with involuntary manslaughter. In another gender-reveal-related tech-fire tragedy, a proud father-to-be US Border Patrol agent packed a "reveal" target with explosives then shot it with a high-powered rifle, causing the massive Sawmill fire which burned 47,000 acres, but luckily resulted in no injuries or deaths. The parents were ordered to pay $8,188,069 in restitution. (It was a boy.)

It Starts with You

With the specter of so many complicated modern apocalypses, you might rightly be wondering: Whose problem is all this after all? Who will have to pay the costs of it? Basically, who owns the risk of the apocalypse? Well, you do. I do! We all do! It's a collective risk that we all share, like it or not. And the most effective way to move forward is to build a community of risk management around the shared understanding that we're all in this together.

Since we all own the risk of the apocalypse, it makes sense to manage that risk together. And we humans have built institutions to help us do just that, including governments, insurance companies, and more informal community-based systems. Unfortunately, these institutions and systems don't always work. Sometimes, they can even make it harder for individuals and communities to prepare for, and recover from, crises. And some can actually create ambiguity about who is responsible in a crisis. When it comes to things like natural disasters or human-caused humanitarian crises, the answer to the question of who owns the risk can be downright fuzzy: Is it

How the World Could End

Swallowed by the Sun

Think we have a bright future ahead? You're right! The sun is actually going to keep shining brighter and brighter until, in about a billion years, it will shine so brightly and emit so much heat that it will turn our oceans into cauldrons of boiling water and totally vaporize life on our planet (according to space journalist Matt Williams, at least). Another four to five billion years after that, the sun's hydrogen core will be depleted and it will become a giant red star, swelling to more than 100 times its current diameter. These are the best predictions we have, given current and imperfect models of the long-term behavior of the sun.

So there *is* an expiration date on our planet. Earth will not be inhabitable in about a billion years. That's a long, long way off, and we'll be damn lucky if we humans stick around long enough to worry about that. Also, if we do make it until then, our civilization will (hopefully) be advanced enough that we'll have a lot more options for dealing with that kind of unbearably "bright" future.

the institutions in place to help deal with risk or is it the people on the ground who have to face the consequences of the crisis?

We know when communities are put in a position where they can make decisions together, it is much easier to manage efforts, resources, and institutional structures to prepare for long-term risks. The institutions created to own some of our biggest risks sometimes don't have the capacity to understand, treat, and mitigate them appropriately, as happened with FEMA in the aftermath of Hurricane Katrina.

Because we need to look at owning the apocalypse on myriad levels, the best place you can start is to consider the ways that you can effectively manage your own risks as an individual and a household. This buys everyone time to figure out how to best handle a given crisis, because people's basic needs will be met if everyone has a shelter-in-place kit, for example. By adapting successful small-scale strategies for large-scale problems, we can begin to make sure our systems are resilient and agile enough so we have the time—as individuals, as households, as a society—to respond effectively when an apocalypse happens, whether it's another pandemic, global fires, a nuclear event, or something else.

The ultimate goal is to create a system that includes neighborhoods, regions, nations, and the global community in a robust and resilient network. Not because households should solely own their risk (there's a lot that should be owned at other levels), but because they can be building blocks for a multilevel system of resilience. And, deep breath, that resilience begins with prepping.

PREPPING PREPS YOUR MINDSET

Having your mind in the right place is not just about having Buddhist monk–level self-control when the world is falling apart around you. It's about having a plan, knowing your exits, and putting some basic preparations (preps) in place. But getting started with preps and a plan can itself be a challenge. Not because it's hard (it's actually pretty easy), but because it can seem like it's going to be really hard.

I had major psychological blocks to getting my apocalypse survival act together for a long time. It wasn't until early 2020,

EVERYDAY CARRY KIT

GO BAG

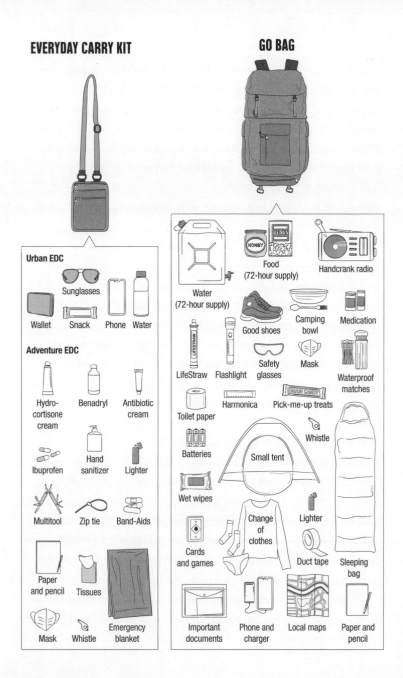

Urban EDC

- Sunglasses
- Wallet
- Snack
- Phone
- Water

Adventure EDC

- Hydro-cortisone cream
- Benadryl
- Antibiotic cream
- Ibuprofen
- Hand sanitizer
- Lighter
- Multitool
- Zip tie
- Band-Aids
- Paper and pencil
- Tissues
- Emergency blanket
- Mask
- Whistle

Go Bag items:

- Water (72-hour supply)
- Food (72-hour supply)
- Handcrank radio
- Good shoes
- Camping bowl
- Medication
- LifeStraw
- Flashlight
- Safety glasses
- Mask
- Waterproof matches
- Toilet paper
- Harmonica
- Pick-me-up treats
- Whistle
- Batteries
- Small tent
- Wet wipes
- Change of clothes
- Lighter
- Cards and games
- Duct tape
- Sleeping bag
- Important documents
- Phone and charger
- Local maps
- Paper and pencil

just before the pandemic apocalypse wreaked havoc on all our lives, that I finally took care of it. At the time, I was with a research team on the Gulf Coast of Mississippi doing fieldwork with the Cajun Navy (a decentralized set of groups made up mostly of fishers, crabbers, and boat hobbyists who organize themselves to help people in the aftermath of hurricanes in the area). We were studying them to understand how and why they risked their lives and spent a lot of their own money and resources saving people after Hurricane Katrina and other storms hit that region. I got to talking with my friend and colleague Keith Tidball, a commander in the National Guard and an all-hazards prep expert (in addition to his day job as a researcher at Cornell), about prepping and disaster readiness, when I admitted that I had yet to put together a go-bag. I told him I was worried that I would do it wrong, or that I would forget something important—which would ultimately doom me in the event of an apocalypse. And that fear was keeping me from getting my basic prepping act together.

Keith looked at me sideways for what felt like an apocalyptically long time. Then he gave me a parental talking to and returned a short while later with his travel medical kit, which I learned he had once used to keep a car accident victim alive until paramedics came. He gave it to me (along with a waterproof container filled with matches) and told me that I now had a go-bag. He then said that when I got home, I should just keep those items in my hiking backpack, which would be my go-bag until I got a backpack specifically for go-purposes. Suddenly I was out of excuses. But now that I had a starter go-bag, it was easy to add more things to it. And it was much easier and more fun than I thought it would be. It was empowering too, and it immediately made the apocalypse seem less scary.

I want to share with you some of this empowering and de-scarifying energy that Tidball imparted to me. I bet that, like me, you'll feel much better if you just get started with a few small preps. So I'm going to channel Tidball here: Something is infinitely better than nothing, so grab an old backpack (or any old bag, really) and do three simple things:

Step 1: Put a first aid kit in there (even if it's just a few Band-Aids and some antibiotic cream in a zip-top bag).

Step 2: Put in a handful of matches in something waterproof (a zip-top bag will do for now).

Step 3: Think back to the beginning of Chapter 2; what was the one thing you'd want to have with you in the apocalypse? Maybe it's a brightly colored towel or a lightweight wool shirt. Or playing cards or some little bottles of whiskey. If you're outdoorsy, maybe you've already got a LifeStraw or water purifying tablets lying around.

It doesn't really matter if you have everything you need yet—what matters is that you get started. When you're feeling ready for more, think about your own unique vulnerabilities and what items can help cover those. Maybe you get hangry easily, so throw in some protein bars. Or you wear glasses that could break so you pop an extra old pair in the bag. If boredom is your worst enemy, a harmonica or playing cards could be a good choice. For me, it's that I get cold easily if I stop moving. The first extra thing I put in my go-bag was some old wool layers. Put those things in your bag and then stow it at the top of your closet or somewhere you can grab it easily. And now you've got a starter go-bag.

Prepping isn't just about being ready for disasters, it is about knowing yourself better, understanding your strengths and vulnerabilities, including those of the region where you live. The more you prep, the more at ease you'll feel with the prospect of disaster—and the more at ease you feel, the easier it is to prep.

EMBRACING YOUR INNER PREPPER

Embracing prepping—specifically all-hazards prepping—is one of the key strategies for surviving apocalypses and avoiding falling down a dysfunctional panic hole. All-hazards prepping means general prepping for disasters, not being ready for every possible apocalyptic permutation. It's about buying time to plan your next steps if a major life- or world-changing disaster happens. With all-hazards prepping, you're also investing in comfort, convenience, and safety in case of more minor or shorter-lived disasters. Think of it as ensuring that your apocalyptic experience will be a more glamp-tastic, deep-pantry party, and less hungry-hungry horribleness.

All-hazards prepping is also helpful in being realistic about the risks you face and prepping for them specifically. For example, do you live where wildfires happen, or could? Then you should have a good go-plan (evacuation plan), a go-bag, and a car kit. Are earthquakes a threat where you are? Start with an earthquake kit and a tent in case you need to camp in your yard afterward.

All-hazards prepping
An approach to emergency preparedness that prioritizes general-purpose preparation and being ready for the most likely disasters in your region. All-hazard prepping has other advantages, including giving you time to assess a situation and plan in the event of an emergency and also reducing the strain on emergency response teams likely trying to respond to the acute crisis.

THE MANY USES OF DUCT TAPE

Duct tape might just be the most versatile and valuable tool known to humankind. In addition to its versatility with repairing things, it's also useful for making things and for medical purposes. You can use duct tape to DIY stuff, like fabricating a little foldable cup for drinking water, or making a rope, a rain hat, or a saddle. You can even use it to (temporarily) close wounds, get rid of warts (nobody knows why this works but it does), restrain unruly zombies, and fix your drunk friend's platform shoes (you're welcome, Sarah!).

I understand that you might be a little reluctant to embrace the whole prepper identity right out of the gate. You might be thinking, *Those preppers are crazy; I'm not like that!* But these days, there are all flavors of preppers, from gun-toting, cabin-living, former military members to sustainable-living-focused Vermonters to suburban soccer parents ready to transform their minivans into go-vehicles at the drop of an apocalyptic hat. Prepping is not just for doomsdayers anymore—it's for everyone! I've discovered that it's for me and I bet—if you give it a chance—you'll find that it's for you too.

Perhaps the most important reason to get prepping is that it can be a fun, meaningful, and empowering way to spend your time. And it can also make your daily life easier! A deep pantry comes in super handy on those hectic weeknights. The paper towels in your car kit might save the day when your nephew has a raging nosebleed in the backseat (did for me). And that duct tape in your everyday carry can fix almost anything that might break while you're out, from falling-apart sneakers on an urban adventure to a ripped backpack on a mountain hike.

Prepping used to be built into our cultural practices, but our modern Western, market-integrated lifestyle puts forth the illusion that we don't need to be prepared. We all drank that collectively comforting Kool-Aid that said there was no need to have supplies on hand in case of an emergency because you can just go to the store. Nor would you need to consider what you'd do in the event of a fire or a flood, because insurance will take care of the damage and surely FEMA or some other government agency will take care of you and your loved ones personally in the wake of a disaster.

But not only is it unwise to depend on institutional power to manage risk on our behalf, it also deprives us of something fundamental to who we are: managing our own individual risk and participating in collective risk management, which are things we have done for as long as we've been human.

Now that you're on board with embracing your inner prepper, where do you start? How do you actually prepare for the apocalypse?

WHY GET YOUR PREPPING ACT TOGETHER?

1 Some basic everyday prepping can make your day-to-day life easier and more fun.

2 Prepping can add meaning and a sense of purpose to your life.

3 Covering yourself in case of emergency can be empowering and anxiety reducing.

4 Being prepared makes you a better Z-team member because you're managing your own risks to the extent that you can.

5 Prepping puts you in a position where you can help others who might be in need.

Avoid the storm

Risk avoidance: Changing what you are doing in order to not take risks or shifting to activities with more reliable returns.

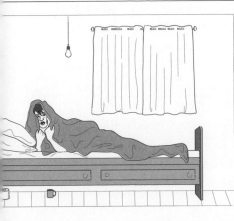

Shelter from the storm

Risk reduction: Investing time and energy to reduce the likelihood or severity of shocks.

Help in trying times

Risk transfer: Sharing risk with others, for example through need-based transfer systems. Risk transfer is the only risk management strategy that requires other people for it to work.

Weather the storm

Risk retention: Also known as "self-insurance," making sure you have enough resources to get through a shock.

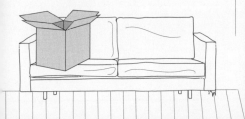

When we look back in human history and across societies, we have a fair amount of insight into the job of managing risk and getting through crises.

Household preps

How can you get your household in order—in a fun and exciting way—to be more ready for apocalypses but also for smaller, more domestic catastrophes? Follow these tips and you'll be well prepared.

Pantry: First, ask yourself: What do you like to eat? How can you actually set it up so weeknight dinners are easier? No need to go to the store or Instacart groceries or Doordash disgusting pizza, because you have everything you need to survive your crazy weeknight dinner apocalypses, all here in your deep-as-fuck pantry!

Figure out what shelf-stable foods you like to have as part of your usual diet and then be sure to have an extra supply of those on hand, always. Then put the newest/freshest food in the back. This makes you more resilient to both the daily kind of catastrophes and the world-ending kind.

Also, some foods will be easier than others to prepare in an apocalypse (or during a rushed weeknight) where you don't have hot water. Couscous (did you know you don't even have to cook it? Just rehydrate and wait! Yes, I discovered this by accident), par-cooked rice/pasta, nuts, and dried fruits and veg are all great pantry stuffers that will help your day-to-day meal management and prepare you for the apocalypse.

PANTRY BASICS

Dry goods

- Dried beans
- Rice (regular & quick cook)
- Couscous
- Pasta
- Quinoa
- Dried fruit
- Nuts
- Coconut oil
- Olive oil
- Nut butters
- Canned beans
- Canned vegetables
- Canned fruit
- Honey
- Sugar
- Flour (white & whole wheat)
- Salt
- Water (not a dry good, but keep in your pantry)

Cleaning & hygiene supplies

- Paper towels
- Toilet paper
- Napkins
- Multipurpose cleaner
- Bleach
- Hand soap
- Shampoo & conditioner
- Deodorant
- Feminine products
- Toothpaste
- Extra toothbrushes
- Floss
- Contact lens solution

Shelter-in-place kit: This is at the heart of your emergency survival plan. It should cover everything you and your family need to survive for 72 hours without leaving the house. In a zombie apocalypse (or a run-of-the-mill pandemic), this is 100 percent your winning strategy.

If you already have a deep pantry, food is the easy part—just put some easy-to-prep long-shelf-life food from that

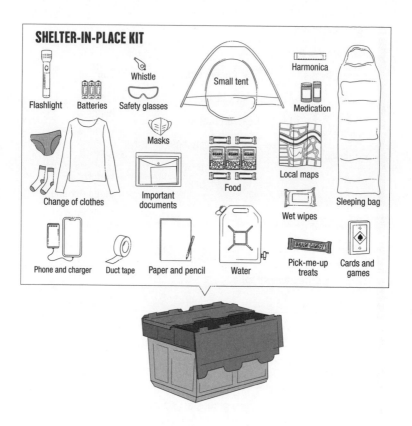

SHELTER-IN-PLACE KIT

Flashlight | Batteries | Whistle | Safety glasses | Small tent | Harmonica

Medication

Masks

Change of clothes | Important documents | Food | Local maps | Sleeping bag

Wet wipes

Phone and charger | Duct tape | Paper and pencil | Water | Pick-me-up treats | Cards and games

pantry into your shelter-in-place (SIP) kit. And if you're deep in cleaning and hygiene supplies as well, grab some of those for your SIP too. You'll also want some extra things, starting with a solid first aid kit and extra medicines (think pain reliever, digestion aids, allergy medication). You can also throw in some basic medical monitoring equipment (blood oxygen monitor), playing cards, and musical instruments, like a harmonica, a ukulele, a tambourine, or an egg shaker.

HOW TO CALCULATE HOW MUCH WATER YOU NEED IN YOUR SIP

Water is easy to neglect. One liter per person per day is the bare minimum. So, take the number of people in your household and multiply that by three to get your 72-hour supply. I'm a fan of 1-liter bottles because it's super clear how much you have and easy to dole out one per person per day, if needed.

On-the-move preps

It's great to have your home well set up in case of an emergency where you need to shelter in place, but being home is not always an option. Sometimes a catastrophic situation necessitates leaving your house, say during a hurricane or a wildfire. Other times an emergency might arise when you're out and about. For these kinds of situations, you need to get your on-the-move preps in order.

Go-bag: If you haven't already, it's time to pull out the go-bag we started on earlier in this chapter (see page 152). You'll want to add some items to the first aid kit and matches that are already there (see page 150).

You should also have a go-bag for each member of your family, including for each of your children, if you have them, and older relatives. Also, if you have pets, you should have supplies in your go-bag for them (see sidebar page 164). And one last thing: I'm a big fan of wool, and you should be too. It'll keep you warm when it's cold, cool when it's hot, and isn't compromised if it gets wet (unlike cotton, which could quite literally kill you if you get stuck out in the cold and rain in it). So get those wool layers into your go-bag—and why not add some to your apocalypse-casual wardrobe while you're at it (see page 194)?

GO-BAGS FOR BABIES AND SMALL CHILDREN

If your kid is big enough to carry a backpack, they should have their own go-bag (see regular go-bag section). But for really little ones, you might want to have a special kit that you carry in your bag with their supplies, including:

- 72-hour supply of disposable diapers and wipes, if you've got a little one still in diapers or recently out of diapers

- If breastfeeding is an option for you, be prepared to—it is much safer than bottlefeeding for babies in disasters. If breastfeeding isn't an option, make sure you have sterilized water and enough formula for 72 hours.

- 2–3 changes of clothes

- Lots of appropriate food and snacks if your little one is eating solids

- Warm blankets

- A high-quality carrier that you can wear while also carrying your go-bag

- Supplies of any medicines, creams, etc., that you or your little one need to be healthy and comfortable

- A few toys/games to keep everybody sane and entertained

You could of course, bring much, much more along with you to keep your little ones happy in the event of an emergency, but there is a trade-off between being agile versus thorough when you're on the move with a very small child. You might want to have an extra bag with all sorts of additional things that you can throw in your car if you have space and know you won't have to be carrying everything by hand.

CAR KIT NECESSITIES

Gloves

Emergency blankets

Food

Water

Jumper cables

Reflective vest

Ice scraper

Wet wipes

Emergency triangle

First aid kit

Hand sanitizer

Wet wipes

Extras

Snow chains

Shovel

Spare tire

Jack

Masks

Toilet paper

Paper towels

Car kit: I love my car kit. From stemming my nephew's gushing nosebleed in the middle of nowhere, Arizona, to doling out Band-Aids to not-so-outdoorsy dates, to jumping my car in a pinch, I'm always grateful to know I have almost everything I could need in a tight little duffel in the trunk of my car.

Everyday carry: I use my everyday carry (EDC) even more often than my car kit. Probably because I take it with me when I'm hiking, skiing, traveling, or going anywhere far from home. The trick to an EDC is to make it small enough to easily take

GO-BAGS FOR PETS

If you have a pet, make sure your go-bag for them has these necessities:

- 72-hour supply of food

- Treats

- Any medicines they need

- Water bowl and LifeStraw filter bottle

- Poop bags

- Paper towels

- Disinfectant

- Leash/collar/harness

- Vaccination history

- Muzzle (in case they get a painful injury and require care, or if they can get bitey when they're stressed)

- Blanket for them to rest on/to keep warm

- A toy or two to keep them entertained

If your pet is hardy enough to carry their own, why not get them an adorable little carry pack for their 72-hour supply?

with you. (Also, just to be clear, when I say EDC I don't mean a weapon. I mean a little kit with stuff that I take with me when there's some chance I might get into a bit of trouble.)

EDC variations: If you really get into EDCs, there are lots of variations you can curate. For example, Tidball has a special EDC for airplane travel with no sharps. Each of us has an EDC for urban days, which is basically what you put in your pockets/purse in the morning before you head out, or what you just (intentionally or unintentionally) leave in your bag at all times.

My EDC is multilayered. It starts with my wallet and phone as my core carry (Night on the town? That's what's in my pockets). My next layer for a typical day includes my sunglasses (with case) and my 16-ounce water bottle. Then I have my "proper" EDC (see page 150), which I take with me when I'm out of my usual comfort zone, including traveling, hiking, biking, skiing, and climbing, but I have an extra add to that: a multitool I clip to the outside so I remember to take it off if I am getting on a plane (because those babies don't fly).

The great thing about these on-the-go preps is that you can tailor them to your specific needs when you're out and about. Do you get flat tires on your bike? Often have car problems? Get hangry? There's a prep for all that. The SIP, EDC, go-bag, and car kit suggestions in this chapter are nothing more than things other people have realized are really important because the need for them arises again and again.

Your own unique preps should come from an awareness of your vulnerabilities—and also your strengths. For example, I'm really good at removing splinters and cactus needles, so I have tweezers and a pen light in my EDC. I also have a thin wool headband that folds up to almost nothing but will keep my ears warm in a pinch, because I know I become completely nonfunctional if my ears get cold.

Managing Apocalyptic Risk Together

Until now we've talked mostly about managing risk as an individual or a household, but we know risk transfers can help us start building a pretty robust apocalypse-ready community. We've also seen how, in many small-scale societies, people work together to proactively manage risk. But managing risk together can be harder when we're embedded in a huge society where we don't have much control over institutional practices and policy decisions. In our modern Western, market-integrated societies—where denial about the risks we face is tantamount to a survival strategy on its own—it's critical that we develop not only a shared understanding of the risks we face but build systems together to manage those risks. The alternative is, well, apocalyptic.

Western societies tend to chronically underinvest in preparedness because we don't properly wrap our collective brains around the problem. Too often, we favor private goods (i.e., stuff we can have for ourselves) over public goods (things that benefit everyone). We can't seem to coordinate our collective behavior to take advantage of the long-term economic benefits of spending on disaster readiness in advance.

"The arc of history does not automatically bend toward preparedness. It must be bent," says esteemed science journalist Ed Yong. In the context of the COVID-19 pandemic, Yong talks about how public health is invisible if successful. And that's the challenge for proactive risk management: When efforts are taken ahead of time to prepare for a problem and they're successful, how do you get people (and politicians) to appreciate that something bad didn't happen? One thing we can potentially do is celebrate when we have near misses that we can attribute even just a little bit to our collective and proactive risk-management efforts.

And there are other reasons to start working together to blunt our risks in advance. Preparing for risks in a community is more satisfying and effective than doing it by yourself. In fact, the very act of doing it together is part of what makes for a sense of community. It can actually help reinforce the fabric of society while increasing our feelings of interdependence with one another.

HOW SMALL-SCALE SOCIETIES SCALE UP HELP

One of the societies we studied in the Human Generosity Project, Fijian fishing villages, scale up their risk-management practices when major disasters strike. On a day-to-day basis in normal times, they help each other out mostly within their own villages. This is based on village membership, meaning that anybody can kerekere anybody else in the village (yes, you can use "kerekere" as both a verb and a noun). This is in contrast to osotua, which is based on one-to-one relationships cultivated over lifetimes. But there is another, higher level of kerekere relationships that exists atop this within-village helping system: Whole villages can have kerekere relationships with other villages, which comes in handy when a devastating cyclone hits. Because these can do so much damage to an entire village that nobody in that village would be able to realistically help anybody else within their own village, being able to kerekere neighboring villages is critical to the long-term survival of these communities.

Consciously or not, Fijians have come up with a solution to preparing for The Big One: They scale up their "insurance" to the village level. And this system has been working for traditional Fijian villages for many generations. Villages consecrate these village-to-village risk-pooling relationships with rituals where they come together and acknowledge the importance of the bond that they share through giving gifts: whale teeth wrapped in rope to signify the "weight" of the relationship.

HOW CHALLENGING TIMES BRING OUT
THE BEST IN US

Wouldn't it be great if we could build a system for managing risk that got better and better as things got worse and worse? Perhaps we can. Systems that get better as things get worse are called antifragile systems, a term coined by Nassim Taleb in *The Black Swan*, a book about those rare events that are impossible to insure against because we just don't know when they might happen, and if they happen how bad they would be.

Need-based transfer systems are a prime example of antifragile systems. If there are shocks and disasters happening, people ask each other for help, new relationships get built, and existing ones are maintained and strengthened. On the other hand, when things are easy and nobody needs

WHAT HAPPENED AFTER THE DEVASTATING FIRES IN MATI?

On July 23, 2018, a devastating fire roared through the seaside town of Mati, just east of Athens, Greece. Within hours, a surreal and apocalyptic envelope of fire had engulfed the town, with flames dropping down from the sky, burning people alive in their cars and homes. Hundreds of people fled to the sea where they waited in thick smoke and blistering heat to be rescued. Several hours later the fire was over, but the community was left shell-shocked. In the days that followed, Mati's youth population sprang into action, helping the community recover from the horrendous event. They brought food and water to people who were hunkering down in what was left of their homes. They coordinated clearing the streets and took to social media, organizing hundreds of volunteers to help. While many of the adults were paralyzed, the younger generation jumped into action without delay, not only displaying unbelievable resilience in this time of crisis, but also contributing to the resilience of their community. These same youth now travel to other areas in Greece in the aftermath of fires to help households and communities recover.

help from anybody, people don't build or cultivate relationships based on assisting each other. During easy times, relationships that could ultimately lead to networks that could provide resilience in the most difficult times don't get built.

Networks based on helping those most in need spontaneously emerge when disasters strike (like those neighbors running extension cords to nearby homes without electricity after Gulf Coast hurricanes, or young people in Mati helping their community recover from the 2018 fire that occurred there). And sometimes they create intense relationships between people who didn't even know each other before things got bad. But to be clear, you really want to have an existing network in place *before* things get bad and you're dealing with the largest and most intense kinds of needs. Building relationships ahead of time means you immediately know who to go to when things get hard. This is how need-based transfer systems in small-scale societies work.

Creating need-based transfer networks that are appropriate for the scale of the disasters we face is one of the most important strategies that we can use to build resilience against our risk. Part of what makes them resilient is their modularity, which can keep shocks from reverberating like they might in a fully interconnected global economy.

BUILDING FOR UNCERTAINTY

A few years ago, as part of the Human Generosity Project, we asked ranchers in the US southwestern desert about the kinds of needs that they faced and also how predictable those needs were. We're talking about things such as broken equipment, illness, and cattle branding. We also asked them if, when they helped their friends and neighbors, they expected to get paid back for that help. We learned that for unpredictable needs— like those that arose from accidents and injuries—people were more likely to say they didn't expect to get paid back for helping. And this is true for modern-day cowboys living on ranches in the desert to people living in cities and suburbs. What this research told us was that an unexpected crisis begets a spontaneous generosity that comes without expectations of being repaid.

SEEING RISK-POOLING RELATIONSHIPS AS SACRED

The scale of the risks we face today is far vaster than ever before in human history. There are more of us alive today than ever before, and the potential catastrophes that loom over us are larger in their reach and longer in their effects than we've ever known. Complicating matters is that we simply didn't evolve to deal with managing risk at global and generational scales.

> In many ways, employing and using modern insurance has become a thing of suffering, rather than one of relief.

But the large size of our problems need not be a barrier to dealing with the prospect of The Big One. In fact, it can be just the opposite if we frame those problems the right way (we all share the same planet, and presumably want it to thrive) and put systems in place that help us avoid the pitfalls of cooperating at the much larger scales (like good systems for detecting and responding to cheating in order to avoid being exploited).

One way to frame things that helps make cooperation more stable and less exploitable is to look at relationships built around

FRATERNAL SOCIETIES HELPED COMMUNITIES MANAGE RISK

An early form of collective insurance was based in the fraternal societies of the 1800s. In these groups, people (usually men) banded together to help each other with unexpected expenses like medical bills, funeral costs, or catastrophic losses from disasters like fires. Although these fraternal societies predate commercial insurance, they have some similarities, such as providing services including health, life, and funeral insurance, sick leave benefits, and the care of orphans of deceased members. People who were part of these fraternal societies contributed small amounts of money regularly to a collective fund that would be available to members who were in need.

These societies (including the Masons in the United States and the Odd Fellows in the UK) had another big draw: They were fun to be a part of. Often, they were an important part of the social lives of the members, regularly organizing festivals, parties, and special events. Even though these societies were typically based on paying dues into a collective fund, they were still similar in many ways to the need-based transfer systems of small-scale societies, which are built on social relationships and maintained through spending time together and building trust.

mutual aid as sacrosanct. For our ancestors, being somebody's backup was a sacred kind of relationship. This was the case for hunter-gatherers, and these relationships continued to be important as we developed agriculture, industry, and even institutions for managing risk. These informal insurance systems are deeply embedded, too, in small-scale societies and cultures as seen with osotua and kerekere. But as society became more complex and market-driven these systems changed and morphed from socially and culturally based ones into more formal systems that used recordkeeping, risk calculations, and explicit payments in exchange for coverage if things turned pear-shaped.

Today, our modern insurance is so entwined with markets that it has no soul. In many ways, employing and using modern insurance has become a thing of suffering, rather than one of relief. In other words, informal insurance systems based on human relationships were transformed into market-based insurance. It happened when societal complexity increased and economic pressures gave rise to new financial instruments for managing risk.

Because we can't quantify many long-term risks in ways that work with market-based insurance, it has become a barrier to effectively managing our biggest apocalyptic risks. The good thing about need-based transfer systems designed for people to help each other when in need is they are specifically made (through cultural evolution, probably) for the unpredictability and uncontrollability of the situations where they kick in. So we already have the tools in our cultural toolbox to deal with The Big One—we're just not using them in an organized way to deal with the shocks and catastrophes we're facing now. But that doesn't mean we can't start!

Cultivating Cooperation

We know that helping in times of need is a cross-cultural pattern across small-scale societies. But what about in the large-scale, market-integrated Western societies that many of us live in today? Is it possible to maintain this kind of generosity and cooperation in an increasingly dense, disconnected, and impersonal world where everyone seems to be apocalyptically stressed? Are we doomed to a fate of cheating, exploitation, and the slow disintegration of the

INTERGENERATIONAL EQUITY

When we decide to do something today, how does that affect future generations? And how do we make decisions about what to do right now, when future generations aren't around yet to speak for themselves? That's the topic at the center of an issue called intergenerational equity, i.e., how can we be fair to future generations by taking their interests into account as we make our decisions now? One of the important realizations to come out of this area of study is that we cannot simply value the well-being of future generations based on "the discount rate" (think of it like the inverse of the interest rate—it's how much we value having something now over having it in the future). Some have argued that we should be valuing the future very highly when making decisions today, with the primary goal of being good ancestors to future generations. I have to admit that I love this idea, even though it may be hard to implement.

social order as the world falls apart? Or can we survive and thrive together in the apocalypse, even if some of us are overprivileged smartphone-addicted urban professionals?

Thankfully, the answer is a resounding yes, we can survive and thrive! If the answer was no, that we're ultimately doomed, I wouldn't have written this book. I would instead be holed up in a makeshift bunker counting out my rations in between bouts of doom-scrolling, slowly becoming more and more paranoid until I had no hope of returning to normal society.

The human capacity for cooperation and generosity is, fundamentally, the key to dealing with the fucked-upped-ness of this moment. Cooperation is also the key to setting up systems that will make us more resilient to the challenges of the future as we face down catastrophic risks and grapple with a rapidly changing society.

MINIMIZE CHEATING

Some of the ways to deal with cheating are to monitor individuals carefully or impose sanctions if they violate the rules. But another way to approach it is to simply set up systems where it's difficult or impossible to break the rules. One way to do that is to give up on traditional account-keeping rules in favor of need-based rules, avoiding the possibility of certain kinds of cheating because there is no loan to pay back—if no one anticipates being repaid, it's not exploitative to not repay them.

Of course, cheating is still possible in these scenarios; for example, if individuals ask for help when they're not in need or fail to help if they're asked and able. But what we've seen in our Human Generosity Project studies is that people tend not to cheat this way—as long as resources are visible to others. This suggests that one way to minimize cheating is to set up agreements to help with clear risk ownership (where everyone knows who owns what parts of what risk),

ENSURING OUR COLLECTIVE FUTURE

Here's a quick-start guide to managing risk in a way that will help ensure that we have a collective future we can all look forward to!

1 Accept the fact that many of our risk-management systems will fall apart in the apocalypse, so market insurance won't single-handedly save us.

2 Take an all-hazards approach to prepping.

3 Buy yourself time to plan in the case of emergency (with your SIP, go-bag, car kit, etc.).

4 Support large-scale efforts to help households prepare (e.g., by supporting cooperative extension programs [see page 176]).

and to also be transparent about what resources everyone has (or at least have a central manager of the system who knows).

GREEN THAT RED ZONE

After disasters, whether they are natural or man-made, like war, people have an inherent desire to engage in greening behaviors or restoring shared community environments. This includes planting trees, creating gardens, and restoring green spaces that might have been damaged. My colleague Keith Tidball, who coined the phrase "greening in the red zone," has seen this happen in numerous post-natural disaster and post-conflict situations, including in the aftermath of Hurricane

If you see your neighbors planting trees after a disaster, you might just want to plant some trees yourself.

Katrina. He saw that people who witnessed their friends and neighbors planting trees and building gardens were more likely to do it themselves. In a computer model he and I made, we found that there was a social tipping point where people seeing others engaging in greening behaviors would lead to a positive sort of social contagion, with it spreading to very high levels even if just 30 percent of households started greening. This positive feedback dynamic means that people who jump into action early to make things better after disasters (for example, by planting trees) can have an outsize influence on the trajectory of the whole community. If you get in there early to help, you make it more likely that other people will get in there too, amplifying your efforts through the infectious enthusiasm you brought for restoring your community.

Invest in cooperative extension programs

Cooperative extension programs are community-serving organizations that are part of land-grant universities. They started during the westward expansion in the United States to help deal with the hazards of frontier life. Now most people think of them as farming support only, but their scope was once much larger. They played an important role in the 1918 flu pandemic, helping communities deal with the challenges of widespread illness and then recovery from the fallout. In fact, cooperative extension programs are where the modern all-hazards approach comes from.

Today, cooperative extension programs mostly function to support the remaining family and community-based farms trying to eke out a living. Their role is important, of course, but there's tremendous potential in retooling them to serve a

SHARE WHAT YOU KNOW

Sharing information is a simple way to build a community of readiness and help everyone around you thrive in the apocalypse. It can start with simply having a chat with a neighbor about the likely risks you share in your region. If we all do this, we could make apocalypse chat the new "talking about the weather." After you're done with this book, pass it along to somebody else. Or share some of the tips from it with your friends, family, and neighbors.

broader role of helping households and communities manage risk. By investing taxpayer money in cooperative extension programs, we can get much more bang for the risk-management buck than by just dealing with the aftermath of disasters— by sending in FEMA or the National Guard. (Though these entities should have a role, those roles should not be at the expense of using government resources to help households prepare ahead of time.) Helping the most vulnerable to be better prepared (as cooperative extension programs could do, with the right investment) is not just the right thing to do, but also a way that we can bolster the resilience of entire communities, particularly rural ones that are depopulating and therefore more at risk.

MULTILEVEL RISK MANAGEMENT STARTS WITH YOU

If everyone takes responsibility for managing some of their own risk at the household level, and if they support their wider communities in doing the same (acknowledging that some people aren't capable of managing their own risk), we'll have a world where each of us understands the most likely kinds of disasters we'll face. We'll also know that we're all probably

A QUICK-START GUIDE TO SCALING UP RISK MANAGEMENT

How do you get started managing risk at scale? Follow these easy steps:

1 Start with your household—put on your own metaphorical oxygen mask first before you help others.

2 Help your friends and family manage their risks; share this book to start.

3 Reach out to your neighbors to build community and talk about the risks you face to develop a common understanding.

4 Look into regional organizations/trainings that will help you up your risk-management game.

5 Support community organizations and cooperative extension programs that help people get prepared who might not have the resources to do so.

6 Support legislation that helps individuals and households manage their own risk.

7 Support global risk-management policies that are proactive and disaster relief systems that are based on pre-agreed rules and are automatically triggered in the event of a disaster.

It's also important to support a government-led emergency response. But for it to work effectively, the first and most important thing is that as many people as possible manage their own risks so organized emergency response (FEMA, National Guard, etc.) can be deployed in a more focused manner.

Household   Neighborhood   Region   Globe

able to survive 72 hours sheltering in place in the event of an acute disaster (like a rapidly spreading pandemic where doing so will likely help *everyone*). When very few people have to scramble for the basics, that means fewer people have to put themselves or others in harm's way just to get food, water, or medical supplies—and it also means that fewer people have to show up as "essential workers" to assist others who are not prepared. Then, whatever government resources are available for dealing with a disaster can be laser focused on the disaster itself rather than having to share attention with the humanitarian crisis it creates. This is not to say that the government shouldn't be helping people in need during a crisis—*it absolutely should*. But ensuring that *all* households are prepped ahead of time means that there will be fewer people in dire need immediately, making it easier for those who are to get help from other households, community organizations, and governmental agencies like FEMA. Helping households be prepared is a lot of what cooperative extension programs (see page 176) are about, so supporting these programs (and learning from them!) is a great place to start.

If we're going to stick around for more millennia, we're going to have to get back to managing our collective risks through cooperation, communication, and coordination, as we've done in various ways for previous millennia.

There might also be some benefits to us as individuals and members of our communities if we think more like insurance and reinsurance companies, but with a soul. What if we ask ourselves about what risks we own? What risks are we taking on for others? We can even talk more with our friends, family, and neighbors about what we expect from each other and under what circumstances.

If we're going to stick around for more millennia, we're going to have to get back to managing our collective risks through cooperation, communication, and coordination, as we've done in various ways for previous millennia. That's the core of our humanity. It can also be really fun if we do it right.

LEARN FROM SMALLER DISASTERS TO PREPARE FOR THE BIG ONE

We can think of small disasters as practice runs for The Big One. When small disasters happen, this is a great time to reassess our communities' disaster readiness and shore up our collective risk management and disaster response.

We can increase our resilience by embracing smaller disasters and learning from them. Denial in the face of small apocalypses will keep us unprepared: We don't know what preps we need unless we realize we don't have them, and sometimes a small disaster is a great way to see where the holes are in your apocalypse prep game. (Do you have enough water for your family for 72 hours? How about a way to stay warm if the power/gas goes out in the middle of the winter?) Embracing these smaller disasters, shoring up our vulnerabilities, and asking for help if we need it helps us build our network so that when shit hits the fan we know who to turn to.

We can use this same approach to making our broader systems and institutions more robust as well. If the power grid goes down, or there's a problem with the water system or a breakdown of public transportation, how can we use those "failures" as opportunities to make a more robust and resilient system that can handle shocks, which will put us in a better position to actually deal with The Big One? Using these smaller disasters as opportunities makes more sense than focusing all our energies on trying to eliminate little disasters (especially if that means stretching our systems so thin that they are more vulnerable to large-scale disasters). These kinds of catastrophes are apocalypses in the ancient Greek meaning of the phrase: They are situations that reveal the inherent risk in the world, and as such they are extremely important opportunities for learning.

MANAGING RISK TOGETHER IS A WAY TO BUILD COMMUNITY

One of the big reasons to up your risk-management game is that the very act of engaging in collective efforts to manage risk helps build community. Managing risk in a community is more satisfying and effective than managing risk by yourself. The very act of collectively managing risk can be an essential part of what makes for a sense of community.

When we work together to manage risk, we end up building a community of interdependence in the process. And as we build that interdependent community, it strengthens our capacity to manage risk together in a wonderfully heart-warming positive feedback loop. The key to solving so many of our problems is to see, appreciate, and cultivate our underlying interdependence: We humans simply cannot survive and thrive without one another.

HOW TO THRIVE IN THE APOCALYPSE

05

Now that we know we've got what it takes to survive The Big One, it's time to talk about how to make the apocalypse fun (yes, fun!) and also part of our everyday lives. This includes being ready for emergencies (i.e., having your preps in order as a relevant and fulfilling part of daily, weekly, monthly, and yearly routines), but it also means embracing our current apocalyptic moment and thriving in it. Thankfully, these goals are surprisingly compatible.

We have the cognitive and cultural tools to help us deal with apocalypses as individuals, as groups, even as an entire civilization. Many of these tools are also how we can make the apocalypse less of a drag. Having fun is an extremely important tool in our apocalypse handbook. In fact, having fun preparing for the apocalypse may have been selected by evolution to help us stay engaged and working together when things get really bad. People and groups who were able to keep risk management as a fun part of their mindset, lifestyle, and culture no doubt had an advantage over those who held fast to denial when they were facing a challenging and uncertain future.

Since I started embracing the apocalypse, my lifestyle choices have steadily shifted from aspiring urban chic to

> **Since I started embracing the apocalypse, my lifestyle choices have steadily shifted from aspiring urban chic to handsome homesteading.**

handsome homesteading. I've traded in my cute heels for practical (yet stylish!) boots, gotten rid of all my even mildly corporate-looking clothes, gone all in with my fermentation obsession (see page 198), and have been outfitting my kitchen,

Apocalypse Casual
A lifestyle characterized by practical catastrophe-ready fashion, all-hazards-preparation-inspired homemaking, deep-pantry enthusiasm, and investment in cultivating communities and cultures of preparedness.

car, and outdoor space so I can enjoy the fun and sense of security that comes from knowing that I'll be okay for a large variety of potential catastrophes. Or at least okay enough to buy myself some time to make a plan. In other words, I've adopted the apocalypse-casual lifestyle.

Apocalypse casual (à la business casual) is about making risk management part of your lifestyle in a way that enriches your life and the lives of those you care about. It's about being empowered to build the life you want given the reality of risk that we all face. It's about helping others achieve that as well—not through

As long as there's somebody volunteering to hold the door so the zombies don't come in (see Volunteer's Dilemma, page 114), everything can be okay, even in the apocalypse.

"visioning" or "manifesting" but by actually shoring up vulnerabilities and addressing inequalities in people's abilities to manage risk. Finally, it's about putting risk management for yourself and your community above the goals of accumulating stuff and status. (Unless it's really practical survival gear and a reputation for being an apocalyptic badass.)

The amazing post-apocalyptic book *Station 11* nailed it by going all in with "Survival is insufficient," a line from a *Star Trek: Voyager* episode. In *Station 11*, a community of wandering minstrels share their joy of the arts in the aftermath of a devastating pandemic that killed almost everyone. We humans need more than just food, water, shelter, and physical safety to be okay in the apocalypse. We need each other, we need art, we need opportunities for self-expression and communication, and we need to feel embedded in a community that has a stake in our well-being. These things are necessary for us to thrive, whether in the midst of an apocalypse or in our day-to-day lives. In this chapter, we'll talk about how we can embrace our apocalypt*ish* times, by shifting our lifestyles and the ways that we see ourselves so we can thrive during The Big One. We'll also take a seriously deep dive into how having fun can help us deal with catastophes and better prepare for them before they happen. We need more than survival to deal with the apocalypse, we need thrival!

But first, let's take a humorous look at all the ways that you can fail to thrive in the apocalypse. Here are some of my favorite apocalypse fails:

Thrival
A state of being where your basic needs are met, you are being your best self in the circumstances you find yourself in, and you have the opportunity to help others and contribute to your community.

INDIVIDUAL STRATEGY FAILS

- Put your stuff in a big pile and get on top of it with a gun
- Get an obscenely big house and lots (and lots) of highly impractical cars—because, cars
- Build an underground bunker and stock it with a year's worth of supplies and then hide out there and avoid everyone
- Go to space

COLLECTIVE STRATEGY FAILS

- Get an authoritarian leader to solve all the problems
- Ignore the problem (see page 36)
- Start a war
- Blame others for the problem
- Blame others for the problem and start a war
- Go to space

Our Apocalypt*ish* Times

An important part of thriving in the apocalypse is embracing a shift in lifestyle. We already know how to do this because all of us have done it! If you've ever moved, taken a new job, had kids, gone off to college, or started a new school or training program, you've had to shift your lifestyle. Maybe you got new clothes, changed your commute, altered your diet, picked up new hobbies, made new friends, or shifted your mindset and priorities in an important way.

We've also shifted our collective lifestyles, so we know how to do that too. In the early weeks and months of the COVID-19 pandemic, we all *had* to change our lifestyles in response to the new threats posed to us. In many ways, I found the early times of the pandemic easier than the long, long tail that has followed. Early on, there was a sense of collective shifting and a shared realization that we had to do things differently. Since I'm the kind of person who thrives in chaos *and* I was able to work from home, it was probably a lot easier for me to quickly adjust to the pandemic lifestyle than it was for many others.

I also went into the pandemic with a preexisting apocalyptic sensibility. Two years before COVID, I organized the first Zombie Apocalypse Medicine Meeting, an academic conference using the frame of a ZA as a way to talk about the many challenges we all face today and will in the future. I was also in the middle of producing the third season of my podcast, *Zombified*, which is about all the things that take over our brains and involves a decent amount of playful apocalypse talk (we have episodes about how to build a Z-team, what to put in your go-bag, how to thrive in chaos, and more!).

So I was already in an apocalyptic mindset going into the pandemic, and my lifestyle was already somewhat apocalypse-ready. I've been a big fermenter for years, and already had my kombucha going, my homemade yogurt, and my sourdough strategy locked in so that it was an easy and relaxing part of my otherwise crazy lifestyle and schedule. I was also just starting to play the ukulele and write/perform comedy, two things that came in really handy for dealing with the social and emotional challenges of the pandemic.

My fashion sense had been moving toward apocalypse casual after a few summers of fieldwork for the Human Generosity Project, which helped me realize how nice it is to just have really practical clothes for any conditions in which you find yourself. As for more general prepping, I was newly getting into it when the pandemic hit, so when reality hit that we were in for a long-term disaster, that hit fast forward on my prepping journey. (For the record, I saw it coming weeks ahead of time and I knew it was going to last months, if not years.)

LIVING WITH THE APOCALYPSE

The first thing to recognize about converting to an apocalypse-casual lifestyle is that shifting to it takes time, energy, and resources. For some people and their household, it can be extremely difficult to allocate anything toward a lifestyle shift because their day-to-day demands are too intense. Over the years, I have spent a lot of time figuring out what made my life easier all around, freeing up my time, energy, and resources instead of depleting them. When done right and thoughtfully, shifting to an apocalypse-casual lifestyle should help you simplify your life, live more frugally and meaningfully, and not put additional demands on you.

Apocalypse casual is about living with the reality of the apocalypse in a chill kind of way. It's about letting go of denial about the world being fucked up (remember, we define the apocalypse as a revelation of risk, not the literal end of the world). This means that little apocalypses can be trial runs for The Big One, opportunities to shift our lifestyles in directions that will make us more resilient moving forward—but only if we embrace them and figure out how to live within them effectively, allowing us to do better the next time. If we remain in denial when disaster strikes and hold out hope that everything will go back to the way it was before, we will miss a huge opportunity to enhance our resilience.

If you're not quite there on embracing apocalyptic times in a chill way, don't worry. What follows will give you the knowledge and tools to move your lifestyle to a place where the idea of a disaster or another emergency doesn't fill you with dread, because you're already living a lifestyle that incorporates readiness into your day-to-day.

THE NEW APOCALYPSE-READY YOU

What's your apocalypse-ready personality? What kind of style and grace do you bring to your particular brand of readiness? There are many different personas/approaches to choose (none of which are mutually exclusive). Do any of these resonate for you? Go ahead, mix and match, try a few on for size.

APOCALYPSE-CORE. You're wearing sensible shoes, you've got your EDC, your clothes have good pockets. You are everyday-emergency ready.

CONFRONTING FAILURE TO THRIVE IN THE APOCALYPSE

If you want to thrive in the apocalypse, try not to fall into traps like:

- Wanting/needing lots of stuff
- Being in denial
- Freaking out
- Worrying that everyone else is going to freak out
- Wanting somebody else to manage all your risk for you
- Perpetually gathering information (i.e., doomscrolling) and never doing anything about it

EVERYDAY HERO. You're not just ready for an emergency, you're ready to jump in and help others during an emergency. Maybe you have a military background or you're a paramedic or a firefighter, or just a brave, caring human.

PREPPER CHIC. You're into practical prepper, cottage-core aesthetics. Maybe you have (nondecorative) jars with rice and beans and pasta and dried fruit lining the shelves in your kitchen, or a deeply Instagrammable apocalypse-ready garage.

URBAN HOMESTEADER. You are growing food in your backyard, on your windowsills, or even inside your house. Maybe you have backyard chickens or are into fermenting stuff like kombucha, radishes, yogurt, or sourdough.

BACK-TO-THE-LANDER. You're ready to get out of Dodge and just buy some land and grow some shit (or you've already done it); fuck capitalism.

HOPELESS HELPER. You're a MacBook-typing, avocado-mashing, fancy-coffee-sipping, city-living person with no preps and no plan for the apocalypse, but you're ready to help if someone else has a plan and will give you direction! (To be clear, if you're this type, you're not really "apocalypse-ready," but you can take steps to get there before shit hits the fan.)

If you identify with any or all of the above, then you're well on your way to being apocalypse-ready and part of an apocalypse-ready community. But there are other apocalypse prep styles much less conducive to thriving in the apocalypse, namely:

ANXIOUS DOOM-SCROLLER. You get that there's a problem (a lot of problems), but you're paralyzed by the fire hose of catastrophes that assaults you directly in the face every night as you scroll and scroll and scroll.

ULTRA-WEALTHY ESCAPIST. You have lots of money so you're paying other people to manage your risk for you, build you a bunker, and/or take you to another planet where everything will be fine.*

NEUROTIC HOARDER. You're freaked out about the apocalypse so you buy lots of preps that you don't actually have the space to store. You're motivated by fear and feel compelled to buy any preps that seem like a good deal, regardless of whether or not you are likely to need them.

PARANOID SHOOTER. Your apocalypse plan? Shoot anything that moves. Because everyone is against you and you can't trust anybody. (Note: This is the most ill-advised strategy. It will not help you survive, and may actually hurt your chances of doing so because you will then become a target for others who don't want someone out there just shooting at everything all the time.)

*This probably won't work, will give you a false sense of security, and make you fear people who might be in genuine need. You will also be breaking norms of helping people in need that naturally arise in times of disaster.

Cultivating your apocalypse style and your unique strengths is an important part of embracing uncertain times so you can thrive in them as the awesome, unique person you are.

The Apocalypse-Casual Lifestyle

For me, apocalypse casual means having my EDC, my SIP kit, my car kit, my go-bag, and a deep (yet simple) pantry. It also means road-tripping, talking to everyone, acoustic jamming, hiking, biking, and being outside a lot. It includes investing in my Z-team, growing my community, and even the act of writing this book. Apocalypse casual is the way that I (and many people on my Z-team) have made it through these apocalyptish last few years.

So how do you get started with your own apocalypse-casual lifestyle? I've got six tenets of apocalypse casual to share with you. We'll go into greater depth for each of them later, but here's a quick-start guide:

1 Adopt the apocalypse-casual mindset

2 Sport apocalypse-casual fashion

3 Embrace apocalypse casual at home

4 Embrace apocalypse casual on the road

5 Build an apocalypse-ready community

6 Cultivate fun and weird apocalypse culture

With these six apocalypse-casual tenets, you'll be ready to thrive in the apocalypse. Let's break them each down further so we can see how we can incorporate them into our daily lives and lifestyles.

Megafloods and Atmospheric Rivers

Flooding is not just a problem in coastal areas. It's a threat for inland areas too, like in many parts of California that are along atmospheric rivers, which are basically rivers in the air, made of water vapor that travels thousands of miles from tropical areas, moving huge amounts of water out of the tropics to places like California where they can create severe weather systems. One atmospheric river, called the Pineapple Express, brings massive amounts of water from the tropics near Hawaii to California. It caused the Great Flood of 1862, an event that, if it happened today, would displace up to ten million people and disable the state for weeks or even months. According to climate scientists, the risk of catastrophic floods because of atmospheric rivers is getting higher every year as temperatures rise. (Fun fact: Insects and various small animals can be transported via these rivers in the sky.)

ADOPT THE APOCALYPSE-CASUAL MINDSET

The apocalypse-casual mindset brings together the ideas of denial-rejecting (see page 41) and risk pooling into a life practice. It starts with accepting that we're living in apocalyptic times, and then leaning into that with a certain joy and energy. It's about not panicking in the face of how fucked up things are (or how fucked up they are becoming), but being ready for a variety of potential disasters and, here's the key thing, making that a fun part of our lifestyles. Ultimately, apocalypse casual is about integrating risk management into our daily lives, building relationships with others around that idea, and having a good time as a part of that process.

SPORT APOCALYPSE-CASUAL FASHION

Apocalypse-casual fashion means prioritizing risk management in your choice of clothing, accessories, and shoes. It also means having your EDC in ready and working order (as your most important lifestyle accessory) so that you're prepared for everyday disasters.

Apocalypse-casual fashion is less a particular style and more about the approach of making sure that your clothes, your shoes, and

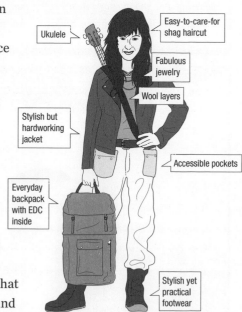

Ukulele

Easy-to-care-for shag haircut

Fabulous jewelry

Wool layers

Stylish but hardworking jacket

Accessible pockets

Everyday backpack with EDC inside

Stylish yet practical footwear

whatever bag you carry won't be huge liabilities if a disaster happens when you're out and about. Here's a tip from go-bag expert Emily Zarka: Keep sneakers in your car if you like to wear heels. And here's a tip from me: Wool is an excellent all-around fabric for your apocalypse-casual wardrobe. It keeps you cool when it's hot, warm when it's cold, and is naturally antimicrobial and odor resistant. Plus, it won't make you cold if it gets wet in a megaflood or just on a rainy walk from the bus stop.

EMBRACE APOCALYPSE CASUAL AT HOME

Embracing apocalypse casual at home involves making risk management part of how you set up your living, breathing, cooking, and sleeping spaces.

Let's start with food. One of the most important parts of the apocalypse-casual lifestyle is to embrace being a practical yet deep-pantried foodie. Begin with a total kitchen game changer: a months-long supply of shelf-stable food that you actually like. This is not just to be apocalypse ready, but also to make busy, daily life much easier. For example, I've learned from deep-pantry expert Erica O'Neil how to stock my pantry with foods I want to eat anyway, stuff that's easy to prepare, and things that are nutritious. Also, if you're into it, you can make it pretty damn aesthetically pleasing for pretty damn cheap.

Apocalypse casual at home goes way deeper than a deep pantry. You'll want to set up your space so you're ready for the unexpected (in a general-purpose, all-hazards kind of way). Do you live somewhere cold? Embrace the fun of getting your firewood chopped, stacked, and ready to go before the cold hits.

Got space for a garden? Plant some stuff—preferably stuff you actually want to eat. Remodeling your place? Why not consider the apocalypse in your design by putting in some extra shelving to hold your deep pantry or setting yourself up with some solar panels, a backup generator, and a battery for your house in case the grid goes down? Interested in fermentation? Get started with some simple lacto-fermented vegetables or yogurt. I'll even help (see page 198).

Another important thing to consider is the overall safety of your living spaces, especially if you have small children who could hurt themselves. Make sure you don't have anything really dangerous in your home: no heavy art that could crash down or empty pools or live electrical wires or the like. If you have guns, make sure they're safely stored. You can find more tips for making your living space safer from your local fire department or resources like Ready.gov.

Once you've got your pantry, your ferments, and your all-hazards apocalypse home situation all sorted, it's time to start simplifying.

Start by asking yourself: Are your belongings helping you manage risk for yourself or your community or are they getting in the way of the apocalypse-casual lifestyle you want? If something isn't doing it for you anymore, you can probably get rid of it or give it to someone who actually needs it. Also, don't forget that cultivating joy is a key part of apocalypse casual, so keep those things that truly bring you joy and incorporate them into your lifestyle in a meaningful way (all props to Marie Kondo here).

EMBRACE APOCALYPSE CASUAL ON THE ROAD

Living the apocalypse-casual lifestyle includes proactively managing your risks when you're on the road, whether you're behind the wheel or sandwiched between two burly passengers on a tiny plane. There's no question that most travel largely sucks right now. But it can be better with a few tips and tricks.

The key is to be intentional about how much you want travel to be a part of your life. There's no need to travel just because you always have or because others expect you to. Rethink what kinds of travel you really want to do and rule out the sort of travel you don't want to do—and then embrace chance if it comes a knockin'. My personal preferences have changed a hell of a lot in recent years. I used to love an all-inclusive beach vacation, but that has become a certain kind of hell for me now. The dripping denial about the reality of the risks we face just about kills me when a "sustainable holiday" means an optional beach cleanup where everyone gets new T-shirts and hats that advertise the hotel as the place for a sustainable beach holiday, and then people pick up seven pieces of trash while taking occasional breaks for shots of tequila to celebrate how much they are helping the Earth—and on vacation no less! I now prefer a more rough-around-the-edges trip with a smaller ecological footprint, fewer programmed activities, and a sense of open-endedness that makes me feel alive.

> Being able to hang with the people you want to weather the apocalypse with is one of the great joys in life.

FERMENTING TIPS!

Supplies

- Lots of Mason or Ball jars in a variety of sizes
- A scale so you can measure things (for sourdough, etc.)
- Fermentation kit with an oxygen extractor, a weight, and special tops (for veggies/fruit)
- Some pop-top beverage containers (for kombucha)
- A glass beverage dispenser with a plastic spout (kombucha doesn't like metal)
- A thermometer (for yogurt)
- A cooler and some hot-water bottles (also for yogurt)

KOMBUCHA

I started my fermenting journey because I got really into drinking kombucha but it was so expensive that I started to worry whether the habit was sustainable or if it was going to drain my bank account and leave me ultimately kombucha-less. Turns out that it's easy enough to make yourself, and my wallet has been much happier.

1 Heat up a kettle full of water and brew some tea concentrate. You'll want about a pint of hot water and 10 bags of simple black or green tea. Add a cup of sugar and mix it all together.

2 After it's cooled a bit, add enough water to make a full gallon of tea.

3 Place the tea into a glass beverage dispenser with 2 cups of plain kombucha and place a SCOBY (symbiotic community of bacteria and yeast; it's a leather-like, pancake-looking biofilm) on top. Don't have a SCOBY? Get one from a friend or order one online!

4 Let it ferment for 10–14 days. You can use the handy beverage dispenser to test it and see if it's to your liking, and then to bottle it when it's ready.

5 When it's tasty, fill up those pop-top bottles and put them in the fridge. Or, if you want to add flavors, you can do a secondary fermentation and add some cut-up fruit, fruit juice, herbs, and whatever else you want to throw in there. Let that ferment for a day or two and then put it in the fridge.

YOGURT

Yogurt is so easy to make that after you make it once you'll be asking yourself why on Earth you've been spending money on yogurt when milk is so much cheaper. Here are the basics:

1 Warm up a pint of milk until it almost boils but doesn't quite (a thermometer can be really helpful for this; you want to get to 180°F).

2 Let the milk cool down until you can stick your finger in for 3 seconds without burning— actually, don't do that; use a thermometer and wait for it to get to around 120°F.

3 Take a ladle or two of the hot (but not too hot) milk and mix it with about a cup of your yogurt starter. This is just to get your starter mixing nicely with the milk before you put it into the rest of the milk. Don't have a yogurt starter? Turns out yogurt is its own starter! All you need is yogurt with live cultures to start.

4 After the starter and ladles of milk are nicely mixed, combine it with the rest of the milk and whisk it.

5 Put the milk/yogurt mixture into some of those Mason jars. Bonus points for warming up the jars ahead of time so that they don't cool down the mixture (you can warm them by running them under hot water or putting them in the oven with just the oven light on).

6 Place your jars into a cooler with two hot-water bottles filled with hot water. This is your incubator. You'll leave your jars in there for 6–12 hours, along with the hot-water bottles, until the texture turns yogurt-y (i.e., if you turn over the jars the yogurt should be gloopy, not liquidy). If it's still liquidy, put it back in your incubator for a few more hours.

Be safe! Before you start fermenting, make sure you know what "normal" should look and smell like. If you have a friend who is also into fermenting, have them show you and teach you. And don't forget to pop online and look at some pics of what is and isn't normal. The internet is a great resource for that. And don't forget: When in doubt, throw it out.

SOURDOUGH

Making sourdough is simpler than it seems, can be made long ahead of time, and doesn't actually require daily feeding. To get started:

1 Mix flour (650g white, 50g whole wheat), water (500g), sourdough starter (350g), and a bit of salt (a teaspoon). Don't have a starter? Ask a friend for one or make your own (I started mine with flour and some kombucha).

2 Let the mixture ferment at room temperature for 3–4 hours, kneading the dough every 45 minutes or so.

3 Split it in two or three loaves and store in round, airtight bowls in the fridge until you're ready to bake it. I like to make mine in batches of three—one loaf the next morning, another a few days later, and then the last one a few days after that. You can store sourdough in the fridge for up to a week, and it gets more delicious and more sour as it rests. Just don't let it go too long; otherwise it will lose its structural integrity.

4 To bake it, preheat a Dutch oven or cloche to 500°F. Cover the dough with flour as you transfer it to a bowl lined with a dishcloth that's been dusted with flour. Let it rise and then put it in the preheated Dutch oven. Bake for 25–35 minutes, depending on the size of your loaf. The bread should be a nice golden brown on top and crispy. After you take it out of the oven, be sure to let it cool a bit before cutting into it; otherwise the texture of the bread will be compromised.

TIP: Take care of your starter by feeding it a mixture of two-parts water, one-part white flour, and one-part whole wheat flour. You really don't need to feed your starter every day unless you're really picky about making bread with a consistent crumb (bread lingo for "texture"). If you are, like me, a little lazy and tolerant of things not being perfect, you can keep your starter in the fridge and feed it about once a week. The cold slows down the rate of growth of the yeast and bacteria, so they don't need to be fed as often. The day before I make a full batch of dough, I'll usually feed the starter to jump-start it a bit. Sometimes I'll let it go a little too long without feeding and I'll have to clean it up a bit, getting rid of the grain alcohol that's accumulated at the top and some oxidized dough—but it has always come back to life fully for me so far. Just don't mess with the mold. If you see anything fuzzy, toss it.

FERMENTED VEGETABLES

Lacto-fermenting vegetables is also ridiculously easy. Especially if you splurge for one of those fermenting kits with a weight, special tops that fit on your Mason jars, and a little tool that lets you pump the oxygen out. Then it is so easy.

1 Slice up your radishes, carrots, cucumbers, cabbage, or whatever you want to ferment into thin slices, and put them in a big bowl with enough salt to coat every surface. Knead the salt into the veggies, let them sit for 20 minutes or so, then drain to remove most of the water.

2 Put the veggies into a big enough jar so that there is room at the top for a weight. Push them down and pack them in as tight as you can. If you used enough salt, it will have made your veggies sweat enough that everything is underwater once you push it all down.

3 Put the weight on, then put on your fermenting top and suck the oxygen out with that clever little pump.

4 Let the jar sit at room temperature for 5–10 days until the flavor is what you're looking for. Don't be afraid to start tasting at 5 days and then repeat step 3.

5 Once you've keyed in the flavor you're looking for, pop a regular lid on your jar and store in the fridge.

TIP: You can dry some of your starter as insurance. Just make a thin layer on a baking sheet, let it dry, and then crumble it and keep it in a plastic bag or mason jar in your pantry. Rehydrate and you've got your starter back.

It's important to think not just about *where* you want to travel, but *how* you want to travel. You can also choose methods of travel that are less stressful and afford you more opportunities to manage your own risk (for example, I prefer road trips over airplane flights now because I like the autonomy of it). I'm also pretty keen on cultivating and maintaining my Z-team, something certainly facilitated by spending in-person time together. For my friends who live far away, travel is the only way to do that. Plus, spending time together is the fun of it—being able to hang with the people you want to weather the apocalypse with is one of the great joys in life.

We all know that travel is filled with increasingly unexpected challenges but also exciting new possibilities. That's part of what makes it fun but sometimes terrifying. The unpredictability of travel also makes it a great place to try out a bunch of your new risk-management skills. For many of us, it is the most likely scenario in which our proactive risk management will pay off quickly.

Here are some tips for various travel scenarios you might choose:

Airline travel tricks

How to be ready for air travel during apocalypses, or anytime really.

- You already know you should travel with just a carry-on if possible. Whenever I have deviated from this sacred rule, I have deeply regretted it.

- Some things to *always* have in your carry-on: change of underwear, change of socks, a T-shirt, basic toiletries, snacks (!!!), masks (even if you're not wearing them on the plane or in the airport, you'll want them in case a new pandemic bursts on the scene while you're traveling), and one warm layer because it can be really fucking cold on airplanes.

- If you're going to any type of gathering, bring at least two test kits for COVID-19 or whatever pandemic is raging by the time you read this (so that you can test yourself as necessary, reducing the chances that you'll inadvertently infect others at any events you attend).

Road trip tricks

How to trick out your vehicle for the apocalypse.

- Start with safety! Do the boring maintenance stuff. Get your car checked regularly, and don't skimp on taking care of it, especially if you're an avid road tripper. Pay extra attention to brakes and tires.

- Learn to do your own maintenance. Check your fluids and your lights regularly, and replace your windshield wipers if they suck because that can interfere with visibility in bad weather.

- Make sure you have your vehicle safety kit locked in, and that you've got twenty-four-hours' worth of water in your car (see page 163).

Boat tricks

How to not die in the middle of the ocean.

- The most important rule of boat safety is don't go out in a boat by yourself if you don't know what the fuck you're doing. And don't go with somebody else who is equally clueless.

- Wear a lifejacket. Yes, I know you know this. Just reminding you.

- Check your equipment. Whatever kind of boat you're using, make sure it's in good working order before setting out.

- Have a map so you know where you are at all times.

- Don't go out in bad weather unless you *really* know what you are doing. And be ready to get out of the water quickly if a storm rolls in on you.

- Bring waterproof layers and warm clothes. Wool and tech materials are best because they keep you warm if they get wet.

- Don't get drunk on the water. It's bad form, it puts you and everyone with you at risk, and it's illegal to operate watercraft under the influence (just like all other vehicles). BUI is a thing and people can get hurt quickly in boats.

- Have a communication plan. Make sure somebody not on the water with you knows where you are and your itinerary. That way, if something bad happens, you have a better chance of getting rescued.

- Bring extra water to drink and more snacks/food than you think you need. Just in case.

On-foot tricks

How to manage risk while backpacking or gliding around a city with a rollaboard suitcase.

- Make sure you're able to move quickly and with agility while carrying your belongings. You need to be able to carry your stuff without help whether you're out on the Appalachian Trail or the streets of Manhattan.

- Carry water and snacks. Again, this is important if you're out in the middle of nowhere or in a city where a quick lunch could blow your entire trip budget.

- Layers! Having a nice layerable wardrobe lets you stay comfortable and thermoregulated wherever you are. Again, I favor wool for the reasons mentioned earlier.

- If you're in a city, please, for fuck's sake, don't stand in the middle of the sidewalk with your head in your smartphone and your rollaboard blocking people walking by as you try to figure out how to get to your Airbnb. It makes you a target, and it's really annoying for everyone who is trying to get by and has no interest in stealing your stuff.

A final thought regarding vacations and the apocalypse: We tend to go on vacation to get away from the challenges of our day-to-day lives, and a little escapism is sometimes exactly what we need. However, too often we return from vacations to lives that simply resume being insanely stressful. But what if we turned holidays and vacations into opportunities to embrace risk management? Rather than taking a vacation from dealing with all the things in our lives (including preparing for uncertain futures), we can incorporate that preparation into our vacations. For example, we can do things like camping, road tripping, having a staycation for deep-pantry development, going to wilderness survival trainings, and traveling to learn about your region and the risks inherent around you. If we think about vacations this way, we might feel better about our day-to-day lives afterward rather than feeling more overwhelmed.

Also, you don't have to travel! If burying your head in the all-inclusive sand is not your idea of a good time, don't go. That kind of scripted holiday is increasingly not for me. Honestly, part of me would rather be filling Mason jars with lentils in my kitchen and feeding my sourdough starter because I want to invest in my future ability to be resilient, not have another mediocre cocktail on a beach. But if that's your thing, I'm not judging—it was once my thing, too. And truly, we're trying to incorporate the apocalypse into our lives by having fun and finding some joy. So, if you want to go on an all-inclusive beach vacation, go for it! And use it as an opportunity to form strong bonds with your Z-team or read an apocalypse book (like this one!) or catch up on ZA podcasts (like *Zombified*!).

BUILD AN APOCALYPSE-READY COMMUNITY

Building an apocalypse-ready community is the beating heart of apocalypse preparation. It's how we build individual-level resilience and also how we need to approach building new systems and institutions meant to keep us collectively safer.

Here are a few specific things *you* can do right now:

1 **Get your DIY apocalypse "insurance."** Manage your risk (see page 147) with your Z-team, your neighborhood embeddedness, and your awareness of regional and global risks.

2 **Share your apocalypse know-how.** Spread the gospel of risk management far and wide! You can simultaneously help your friends, family, and yourself by sharing your knowledge and skills with others. The better your network is at managing risk, the safer everyone will be in the event of an emergency.

3 Improve the systems in which you're embedded. We can change the systems we participate in to strengthen them for dealing with the apocalypse, from cultivating new economic models, to revitalizing cooperative extension programs, to simply building informal risk-pooling relationships in our communities via apocalypse parties (see page 217). Find the level that feels right for you and work on it, but remember: You don't have to do all the things.

4 Support organizations that are working to reduce catastrophic risk. There are lots of smart, interesting people out there who see the reality of risk we're facing, and some have organized themselves into groups aimed at educating and/or enacting practical change for a better future. The Consilience Project, the Center for Existential Risk at Oxford, the Global Futures Lab at ASU—each of these organizations is working to understand and manage the kinds of world-ending risks that keep us all up at night. (For more information, visit: workman.com/afieldguidetotheapocalypse.)

There are lots of things broken with the larger systems we all inhabit, but implementing a lot of these solutions doesn't require tearing these systems down to get them started. We can start small, in our own families, neighborhoods, and communities. And we can also start redefining our relationships with each other, with corporations, regional governments, small businesses, cities, states, and even nations. Systems based on the principles of need-based helping are like little seeds that can be planted within the largely market-driven world that we live in. And they will grow into lively and lovely communities as we all start to see and feel the benefits they give us, both psychologically and practically, as we build resilience to the uncertainties and shocks of apocalyptic living.

CULTIVATE FUN AND WEIRD APOCALYPSE CULTURE

We humans are pretty damn good at making scary things fun through shared experiences, rituals, events, and stories. So the last tenet of apocalypse casual is to make apocalypse readiness part of our culture by incorporating it into the fun things that

A GIFT-GIVING GUIDE FOR THE MODERN PREPPER

What to put in holiday stockings (EDC and go-bag swag):

- Emergency blanket
- LifeStraw
- Water bottle
- A lighter/matches (don't give these to little kids, please)
- High-calorie snacks (you're probably putting these in anyway)

- A harmonica or an egg shaker
- Duct tape
- Band-Aids
- Facial tissue mini packs (These are great literal stuffers—don't be shy about putting in a lot of these!)

Best apocalyptic gifts to spread risk-management cheer:

- Mason jars filled with pantry basics to jump-start their deep pantry
- Multitool
- First aid kit
- Solar charger
- Hand-crank radio

- Wool socks or underlayers
- Easy-to-play musical instruments (see page 223)
- If you want to go all out: starter go-bag, SIP kit, or car kit

we all do together, including parties, festivals, holidays, and other gatherings where we can share information, reduce anxiety, and build community.

Living the apocalypse-casual lifestyle is not just about doing the work in your daily life, but embracing the fun of building community around the culture of apocalypse readiness and awareness. And you know the best way to do that? With a fabulous apocalypse party.

The point is not to party like it's the end of the world, but rather to party together to get on the same page about feeling empowered to do something together. Dealing with the apocalypse is not something that we should relegate to the dark recesses of our minds and cultures; it should be something that we actively embrace, something that we cultivate and invite to the holiday table.

Winter holidays

If we look at the cultural history of many holidays, a lot of them have roots in and around risk management, and the celebration of doing it well. Perhaps the best examples of this are winter holidays, which were originally about feasting in celebration of making it through the winter—something that certainly required careful planning and preparation.

Loads of societies around the world have special winter traditions with roots in risk management. For example, Korean Kimjang gatherings are focused on prepping and storing kimchi (deepen that pantry!) and, according to UNESCO, Kimjang "reaffirms Korean identity and is an excellent opportunity for strengthening family cooperation." Then there's the Icelandic Thorrablot tradition of throwing a big party and feasting on delicious preserved delicacies like fermented shark (tried it, kind of liked it, but my gut microbes weren't as enthusiastic as my tastebuds). And winter solstice traditions from many societies are deeply tied to the challenges of surviving the winter. People monitored their winter reserves, slaughtered (and feasted on) animals before the depths of winter so they wouldn't have to worry about keeping them alive through the coldest days, and enjoyed the fermented beverages and foods that were finally ready to consume after the autumn harvests.

There's no reason why we can't bring some of these risk-management vibes to our winter holidays, even if we're living in market-integrated societies where we can just stroll over to Safeway anytime we're running low on Ben & Jerry's or White Claw. We can embrace the apocalypse a little bit by turning the holidays into a celebration of how we've prepared and use them as yet another opportunity to shore up our vulnerabilities. We can take the time to make sure our pantries are well stocked for the winter (or any other hazardous seasons specific to your region). We can eat and drink foods that we've cultivated ourselves or received from our risk-pooling partners. Go ahead, share some of your sourdough bread, freshly fermented yogurt, or locally picked grapefruit marmalade (thanks Julie!) with your neighbors and Z-team. And by spending quality time with our family and friends, we strengthen those relationships we already have and likely build new ones too.

And it wouldn't be the winter holidays without a bunch of unnecessary stuff changing hands. If you want to opt out of the super-commercialistic stuff-buying extravaganza, risk management can be a great mindset when deciding what to buy to add some apocalyptic holiday cheer. Start by making sure the basics—shelter, water, fire/warmth, and food—are covered for you and your loved ones. Then consider helping out those not as fortunate as you by covering some of those basics.

If you and your family are into the overflowing bounty of stuff during the holidays, channel your fervor into a bunch of go-bag or SIP kit gear that you may have been putting off. Not sure what to get for your friends or family? Figure out where they are in their risk-management journey and help them get to the next step by sending them a hand-crank radio or popping by their house with some apocalypse-casual Mason jars with lentils, quinoa, and pastas to jump-start that deep winter pantry. And for those who hang stockings by the fire with care, instead of filling those stockings with fidget spinners and chocolate Santas, try go-bag multitools and lightweight rations.

Holidays of death and horror

We humans love a good death party. That's why many societies around the world have holidays celebrating death, the dead, and the many other things in the world that are scary. The Mexican holiday Dia de los Muertos is about embracing the tragedy of losses and having a big party while doing it. My colleague Mathew Sandoval pointed out that this holiday has grown and changed in response to the death and trauma that communities have been through, and that it offers an essential space for people to process those losses together. It also gives them the opportunity to be a part of a fun and exuberant community at the same time. We would do well to bring some of that energy to our excessively candy-centric Halloween celebrations.

Valentine's Day

If we think about our most important relationships in terms of risk pooling rather than just romance (see how to date in the apocalypse, page 225), it gives us a chance to look at Valentine's Day differently. We can reclaim the holiday for relationships built around mutual aid and care, whether they are romantic or not. Rather than just celebrating traditional couple-only love, we can celebrate all the relationships we have with people who we know we can depend on in times of need.

Will you risk pool with me?

Kids' parties!

Even though we usually try to protect kids from the idea of bad things out there in the world, many kids are inherently drawn to frightening, even gruesome things; they are morbidly curious (see page 48). In fact, kids are more okay with unexpected risks and catastrophes than most adults. For example, kids who get lost in the woods usually do better than adults because they tend to find a safe spot and chill, while adults usually freak out and expend a bunch of energy getting more lost. As many parents will tell you, kids are more resilient than we give them credit for.

What do experts say about what kids can handle when it comes to the horrors of the end of the world? Coltan Scrivner, an expert in morbid curiosity, pointed out that many kids thrive on scary play, and that it can actually help them deal with anxiety. In fact, there is a cool horror video game called MindLight that has been found to be just as effective at reducing anxiety symptoms as cognitive behavioral therapy (the current gold standard for therapy). And as you might expect, kids like it way more. Scrivner also shared that kids often spontaneously create games that capture their anxieties and concerns about what's going on in the world (for example, making up pandemic-related games during the COVID-19 pandemic). Maybe they can teach us something about making games that help us work through the apocalypses we're trying to deal with.

If you're planning an apocalypse-themed kids' party and inviting the scary to the table, there are some things to keep in mind to make sure it will be fun for everyone. Not all kids are as game for the apocalyptic stuff as others. And kids get scared more easily than adults in general, so keep it playful, fun, and interactive. Instead of clowns and magicians, perhaps invite wilderness medicine doctors, go-bag specialists, deep-pantry experts, and survivalists (less scary than clowns!) to share fun skills (like wilderness first aid), engage kids with interactive activities (how do you build a shelter in the woods?), and even provide some starter supplies that can go home with everyone in those little post-party goody bags (look, mom, I got an emergency blanket!).

Here are some dos and don'ts for making sure it ends up being fun for everyone all around:

DOS:

- Let other parents know what you're planning.

- Pay attention to how kids are responding and be ready to talk or scale things back as needed.

- Make it fun and a little silly to keep the edge off.

- Give plenty of opportunities for learning and actionable ways to manage risk.

BEST APOCALYPSE PARTIES

If apocalypse parties are your thing, you're in luck. There are a multitude of options for you to choose from, many of which incorporate an apocalyptic vibe, fun music, and humans in a generous frame of mind. Some of them also have drugs, chaos, and even talks by scientists and scholars. Something for everyone!

Large-scale apocalypse parties:

Burning Man. Join fifty thousand people in the harsh Nevada desert for a big bohemian party based on self-reliance, gift giving, electronic music, crazy art, and . . . frankly . . . lots of drug use? If that sounds like fun, then Burning Man might be for you. I've never been but I hear it can be a great time. "Baby Burning Mans" have popped up all over: Saguaro Man, Afrika Burn, Korea Burn, Burning Japan, MidBurn (Israel), Kiwiburn, or Nowhere, Spain (where burning is banned due to the threat of wildfire).

Woodstock. Initially conceived as a money-making venture by a group of ambitious music promoters, the 1969 Woodstock Music and Art Fair in Woodstock, New York, morphed into a financial flop but sent a strong message that war was intolerable to a new generation of more than half a million people who valued peace, love, and unity. It took place two more times, in 1994 and 1999, but was never the same.

Dia de los Muertos. The "Day of the Dead" (see page 211) is, in reality, a celebration for the living. The festivities originated with Mictecacihuatl, the Aztec Lady of Death, who invited loved ones to return to the land of the living. Homemade altars (or ofrendas) are piled with toys and sugar skull candies for the departed children, with books, photos, food, and alcohol for the departed adults.

Siberian Yup'ik parties. At the end of a long winter, the Siberian Yup'ik, a North American people, find pause for all manner of celebrations when they welcome the return of wild game or seek nature's blessings for those needy or sick. Yup'ik storyteller Chuna McIntyre explains, "We implore the animal kingdom to help us in our survival because we cannot do it ourselves. We need the animal kingdom, in concert, to survive. So we were constantly in supplication to the natural world to provide us all of the bounty we know nature can give us. But we have to remember not to just take, we have to give. So what we give in return is a ceremony. We give in supplication. We give in song, we give in dance."

End of the World Festival, the Pit, Ukraine. The Pit is (was?) a postapocalyptic festival in Ukraine. The last event held in a pit in Kyiv in 2019, was canceled in 2020 due to the COVID-19 pandemic, then canceled again in 2021 and 2022—because of the Russian invasion. I suspect a festival that includes tours of the Chernobyl nuclear zone has lost its entertainment value given everything else that's going on there.

Wasteland Weekend. Billed as the world's largest postapocalyptic festival, thousands of costumed "Wastelanders" become players in a replica *Mad Max* movie set in the Mojave Desert in California. Their goal? To use creativity, play, interaction, and inspiration to build the future world they desire. There's an epic car cruise with more than 100 apocalypse core-styled bikes and buggies, mini-robot battles, nightly contests in the Thunderdome, and a postapocalyptic bathing suit competition. (What's that, you ask? Think *Mad Max* meets *Sports Illustrated* swimsuit issue.) Fittingly, the music lineup has included underground metal band Dead by Wednesday, old-school punk band Soldiers of Destruction, and Portland's Dead Animal Assembly Plant, whose 2021 album, *Bring Out the Dead*, is described by festival organizers as taking "listeners through the different layers of hell."

Junktown, Czech Republic. Under the banner, "Let's create the worse [*sic?*] world together," this Czech postapocalyptic festival attracts about one thousand people a year to a former military base—now a nature preserve. Organizers call the four days of role-playing, music, contests, food, and weapon sales "a passionate tribute to the cult of *Fallout* and *Mad Max*." After a few years' respite, the festival returned in December 2022 as the Junktown Winter Apocalypse.

Apocalypticus V: Road to Ruin, United Kingdom. The call to action: "Attention all Armageddon Wastelanders, Zombie Apocalypse Marauders, and Mad-Max Petrol heads!" This UK human extinction event bills itself as "a springboard for other tribes to join us before dispersing out with a plan to . . . and re-establish humanity." With base camp fittingly adjacent to a military base and a rocket fuel factory, the event highlight is inarguably a concourse of destruction that winds its way through the English countryside.

Oldtown, Poland. In Oldtown, the live action role playing (LARP) is strong and the story is serious. Set in a sun-scorched abandoned Russian airport, hundreds of festivalgoers from all over the world converge to create a dystopian world. As the story goes, the world is incinerated by an atomic fire in October 2077 and the Great War begins. Homes are turned into dust and the Earth's surface becomes a hostile hell. Survivors are hiding in underground bunkers or remote, out-of-the-way locations. Festivalgoers create their character and remain in costume for the full four days, struggling to avoid mutated animals, hungry humans, bandits, and warring factions. But it's not without hope, as some altruistic folks work to rebuild culture, entertainment, and knowledge. The story continues from year to year.

Mind Under Matter Campout Festival. Comedian Shane Mauss started this festival in 2022 in Raleigh, North Carolina, to bring together musicians, comedians, and scientists to have fun and at the same time grapple with the challenges of the apocalyptic times we are living in. From there, this festival has grown to include a fun survivalist element and involvement from apocalypse-minded scientists (like me!).

Zombie Apocalypse Medicine Meeting (ZAMM). Launched in 2020 by the Zombie Apocalypse Medicine Alliance and ASU, ZAMM arose from scientific interest in the unintended biological, technological, and social consequences of host-parasite interactions. ZAMM attracts scientists, artists, doctors, lawyers, ethicists, and futurists from the world over to wrestle with understanding the challenges of zombification and our increasingly apocalyptic present and uncertain future. (Also: I started this meeting, so it's kind of my weird apocalypse baby.)

DON'TS:

- Hire a bunch of actors to terrorize the children.

- Make it simultaneously a surprise party and an apocalypse party.

- Talk about all the ways the world could end and then put the children on the spot about their survival plans.

DIY apocalypse parties

You don't have to wait for a kid's birthday party or a holiday to start having fun getting yourself and your community more prepared for the apocalypse. You can have a prepping party whenever you want. This can be a chance to share what you know with your community, to teach each other apocalypse skills, and to start building relationships that you can depend on when things get tough.

Here are some ideas and themes for apocalypse parties:

POWER'S OUT SLEEPOVER CHALLENGE. Hit the breakers and see—can you and your closest friends survive the night with no power and only the things in your SIP kit? It's fun and a great drill for the real thing!

DEEP-PANTRY DINNER PARTY. Six couples, four hours, one deep pantry. Roll the dice to see whose house you're going to for dinner. Once you get there, work together to make the most delicious meal you can from only the shelf-stable items stored in the pantry. It's a great incentive to stock your pantry deeply and a fun way to share your apocalypse cooking know-how (and learn from your friends).

GO-BAG VACATION. Can you survive for 72 hours with only the contents of your go-bag? You and your two closest friends grab your go-bags and head to the airport. Get on the next flight out of town with nothing other than your go-bag—and no cheating by packing it for vacation.

WILDERNESS MEDICINE LARPING CAMPOUT. Get out into the wilderness for a combination LARP game/wilderness medicine practice party. If you're a game master, make up an adventure that requires players to enact basic wilderness medicine skills like cleaning out and dressing a wound, splinting a broken bone, or—if you're feeling adventuresome—amputation practice (you can use a Gigli saw and a lamb leg from the butcher for this—for real, it's fun!).

SOCIALIZING: HAVING AN APOCALYPSE PARTY

Stimulating conversation
Sharing information and building trust

Sharing food
Opportunities for bonding

Music
Bringing people together around stories and songs

ACOUSTIC APOCALYPSE JAM NIGHT. What's the music of the apocalypse? I'd say any music that is inviting, inclusive, and can be played in front of a fire without amplification. I love bluegrass, folk, and alt country, whether it's the apocalypse or not. Or whatever you want to play, really. Build your jamming skills by hosting or participating in an acoustic apocalypse jam night. Play all apocalypse songs, all unplugged. Tip: It helps to have two or three people who actually know what they're doing around an instrument and/or can carry a tune.

FIRE KEEPER. Go out camping in crappy weather with a few adventuresome insomniac friends; see if you can start a fire using only what you have in your go-bag and keep that fire going all night long through rain, sleet, hail, or snow.

APOCALYPSE SKILLS CHALLENGE. Grab your favorite wilderness survival book (and one that makes sense for your region/ ecology), and head out into the wilderness with a few friends to see how many skills you can master in 24 hours. Can you make a fire with a bow drill? Twine from yucca? Find enough water to sustain yourself?

The music of the apocalypse

One of the best ways to thrive in the apocalypse is to embrace music. Maybe you can play and sing, maybe you don't know how but want to learn, or maybe you like to listen but completely lack musical talent. Regardless of your relationship with music, I hope these tips will be helpful!

The best instruments for the apocalypse are acoustic instruments that are easy to transport.

HOW TO BE PART OF A JAM

Bring a song or two that you can sing and play reasonably that is somewhat well-known so others can join in and it's not just you singing/playing.

Judge the crowd and don't bust out jambusters (songs that are way too hard in terms of chord progression or rhythm for people to be able to play/sing along).

In a well-functioning jamming community, people take turns picking songs, usually going around clockwise with each person picking one song. This gives everyone a chance to offer something up.

If you have the floor, don't keep it as long as possible—jamming is about making music *with* people, not having an audience. I've had the good fortune of meeting many wonderful musicians and community-builders through the bluegrass community, and I've learned most of what I know about jamming from Julie Sullivan-Brace, one of the founders of the Pickin' in the Pines festival in Flagstaff, Arizona, and the brains behind the Roots and Boots Music Camp, which teaches adults and kids alike how to play bluegrass music as part of a community.

Here are some of the dos and don'ts I've picked up from Julie.

Dos:

- Play in the keys of D/G/A/E, ideally. C/F/B flat are okay too.

- Take turns picking what song to play (go around the circle).

- Choose songs that people are likely to know and that are simple.

- If you're up, explain the key and chord progression before you start.

- Do your best to play along to the songs other people pick.

- Offer people the opportunity to solo in between verses (it's good form to go around the circle offering people the chance to solo).

Don'ts:

- Don't play in obscure keys or tunings.
- Don't dominate the jam with your songs.
- Don't veto songs other people pick (see above); try your best to play or just listen if you can't.
- Don't treat everyone else in the jam like they're your backup karaoke track (i.e., don't sing and play all the licks like you're the lead; share the spotlight!).

General apocalypse jam songs and suggested key:

- "Bad Moon Rising," Creedence Clearwater Revival (D)
- "Paradise," John Prine (G)
- "Long Time Gone," Darrell Scott and Tim O'Brien (G)
- "Long Violent History," Tyler Childers (G)
- "Revolution," The Beatles, (A)*
- "Rattlin' Bones," Kasey Chambers (Am)*
- "It's the End of the World as We Know It (And I Feel Fine)," R.E.M. (G)*
- "Watch it Fall," Billy Strings (C)*
- "Apocalypse," Cigarettes After Sex (F)*

Songs for dealing with death:

- "I'll Fly Away," Albert E. Brumley (G)
- "St. James Infirmary," Irving Mills and Don Redman (Am)*
- "Only the Good Die Young," Billy Joel (C)*
- "(Don't Fear) The Reaper," Blue Oyster Cult (Am)*

Mutual aid and cooperation songs:

- "Lean on Me,"
  Bill Withers (A)
- "Stand by Me,"
  Ben E. King (C)
- "One Love,"
  Bob Marley (C)

- "Imagine,"
  John Lennon (C)
- "What a Wonderful World,"
  Louis Armstrong (F)*

Movin' songs:

- "A Lot of Movin',"
  Avett Brothers (G)
- "L.A. Freeway,"
  Guy Clark (G)
- "Free Fallin',"
  Tom Petty (F)*
- "California Stars,"
  Billy Bragg & Wilco (A)*

- "Look at Miss Ohio,"
  Gillian Welch (F)*
- "My Church,"
  Maren Morris (A)*
- "Wildflowers,"
  Tom Petty (F)*

Fun togetherness songs:

- "Shanty,"
  Jonathan Edwards (G)
- "Jambalaya,"
  Hank Williams (G)

- "Drinkin' Dark Whiskey,"
  The Steeldrivers (G)

Another thing that's great to know is some basics of how music like this works. There's something called the circle of fifths, which basically shows how all the chords in Western folk, rock, country, pop, and many other genres of music fit together. Knowing this will help you figure out what the chords are in a song even if all you know is the key that it's in. Cool, huh?

*You'll need to pick up a few more chords to be able to play these songs.

- **UKE.** It's easy! Check out the illustration for the six chords A, Am, C, D, F, G) you need to get started.

- **HARMONICA.** If you get a harmonica in C, you can play along with songs in C or play what's called crossharp with songs that are in G. That basically means drawing in the air rather than blowing out and focusing on the low notes (thanks to my colleague Mike McBeath for these harmonica tips!).

- **GUITAR.** Harder, but not so, so hard. The six chords you need to play most of the songs on the previous pages are all in the illustration.

- **TAMBOURINE.** All you need is a vaguely okay sense of rhythm for this one. Just don't overdo it. Really, you should only play for half the song. Like during the chorus but not the verses, for example.

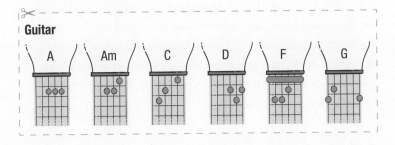

Guitar

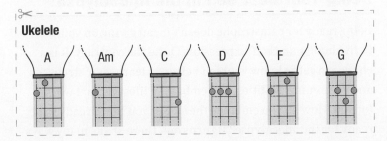

Ukelele

- **EGG SHAKERS.** Great for kids and anybody who can't hold a tune or play a "real" instrument.

- **COWBELL.** Please only play this if you can hold a beat and understand that "more cowbell" doesn't mean all-the-time-as-loud-as possible cowbell (see tambourine warnings). The cowbell can double as a dinner bell, early-alert system, and any number of other functions, with the potential for great all-around functionality but also great potential confusion (Is it dinner time or are the zombies invading?).

- **CAJON.** A nice general-purpose percussion instrument. But if you're coming up on an all-acoustic jam, you'll have to keep it on the quiet side so you don't drown everyone out with your mad beats.

The best music for the apocalypse is not a single style or topic. You can go with apocalypse subjects, mutual-aid topics, on-the-road tunes, fun togetherness jams, and revolution and social change themes. And you'll find plenty of folk, country, bluegrass, rock, pop, and other styles of music that can keep your spirits up, or at least align your apocalypse-embracing spirit with those around you.

Being Your Best Self in the Apocalypse

Being ready for catastrophe doesn't mean giving up your individuality and self-expression. Quite the contrary. It is a chance to get to know yourself better, to learn your strengths and your vulnerabilities, and embrace a lifestyle that works for you. How do you embrace the side of you that's ready to be ready for the apocalypse? It turns out, there are as many ways to thrive in the apocalypse as there are to order a latte.

HOW TO DATE IN THE APOCALYPSE

Dating is hard enough in easy times, let alone apocalyptic ones. Regardless of whether you consider yourself single, part of a couple, or in a nontraditional arrangement, you've probably found that dating is kind of different when the specter of the apocalypse is upon us. You might look at your current partner—or a prospective one—through the lens of how they would fare in a catastrophe. In the apocalypse, Z-team skills come to the fore. Being able to make a decent fire (I'm solidly mediocre at it), having some musical talents to be deployed around a fire (I can hold my own, but I'm no expert), or having general-purpose know-how about managing risk (I got this one!) becomes more important than the classic dating-app propositions, such as how much you like tacos (so much!), whether you think a hot dog is or isn't a sandwich (it is), and how you feel about pineapple on pizza (why the fuck not?).

WYLDFIRE
Embrace apocalypse dating

John M. 📍 **2 miles away**

- ♥ Alluringly adventurous
- ♥ Tantalizingly practical
- ♥ Stimulatingly funny
- ♥ Sensual knife skills
- ♥ Sultry campfire cooking skills
- ♥ Sick zombie combat skills
- ♥ Seductively positive in all situations

The fact is, in this modern world we live in, love and dating still follow pretty traditional scripts that basically come down to: You're looking for the one person with whom you're going to manage 90 percent of your risk. For some people this might make sense, but for many of us that's putting a lot of our eggs in one fairly small apocalyptic basket. Throughout our evolutionary history, we humans have been embedded in rich networks of family and friends with whom we've managed risk. And now we're largely expected to find a virtual stranger and—after a getting-to-know-you period—go all in with them in pretty much every way, often including combining finances, planning lives, and having kids. We're talking super-intense levels of interdependence here. (And, unfortunately, the potential for mutually assured destruction if we do things like get married and have kids—and then things don't go well.)

Now, there's nothing wrong with this kind of going-all-in with somebody. And I'm not going to deny that there's something ridiculously romantic about throwing caution to the wind and falling in love so hard that you want to entwine your life with somebody else in every way, establishing the kind of interdependence that makes it hard to tell where you end and your partner begins. But we might want to rethink the idea that a life partner also has to be a 90 percent risk-management partner. Having just two people is not a great way to set up a resilient risk-pooling network. But it's often the default assumption that that is what a life partner is. (Unless you're lucky enough to be embedded in a huge family and friend network with people who are deeply involved in your life—though this can come with its own challenges). The nice thing is, though, you don't have to go with the default assumptions about dating; you can do what is right for you and your situation.

Whether I'm dating or investing in my friendships, I want to be cultivating relationships with people I would want on my Z-team. I'm definitely looking for somebody with apocalypse awareness and skills, somebody who will be there for me in times of need—apocalyptic or otherwise.

HOW TO WORK IN THE APOCALYPSE

If dating is hard in the apocalypse, working is harder. It can be a challenge to stay motivated and focused, and have that all-important sense of fulfillment when our jobs might not be 100 percent aligned with our goals. How can we manage our careers, the expectations at our jobs, and the need for a work-life balance in these apocalyptic times?

Here are three tips to help guide your thinking:

1 Choose a career that is flexible in terms of where you work, how you work, and time off so that you can be more personally resilient in the apocalypse (note: this isn't an option for everyone because of many inequalities).

2 Consider ways to bring fun risk-management practices into the workplace.

3 Choose a prosocial apocalypse-risk-reducing career. If you're thinking that the end of the world is an important enough thing to spend your life trying to prevent, then you might want to choose a career where you can help make the apocalypse less likely—or at least less catastrophic. There are a bunch of communities of people out there doing just this (see page 207).

Learning to Thrive in the Apocalypse

Thriving in the apocalypse requires that we embrace learning and cultivate a next generation of enthusiastic, apocalypse-resilient young people. This might not be as hard as it seems at first because, when it comes down to it, learning how to deal with the apocalypse is a pretty damn motivating imperative, whether you're an old dog or a spring chicken. When the stakes are high (like our collective futures) it's easy to learn new skills that could help you survive, pay attention to information that might help you understand the problem(s), and collect new tools for working together more effectively to solve the problem(s). We all have what it takes to learn how to thrive in the apocalypse. This is and has been part of who we are as humans since our earliest days.

CHILDREN OF THE APOCALYPSE

A big worry for me and many of my apocalypse-aware parent friends is how to take care of kids in these apocalyptic times. One of our deepest evolutionary impulses is to protect our kids, and saving them from catastrophes is pretty much first on the list. It can be immensely frustrating for parents and alloparents when a child's evolutionary impulses (including morbid curiosity, see page 48) encourage them to take risks and put themselves in harm's way, unnecessarily.

Alloparent
Somebody who takes care of a child but is not the biological parent of that child.

A kid's main job, in a deep evolutionary sense, is to learn about the world. And the most important tool they have in their toolbox is to have fun. Ironically, one of the best ways to help them figure out how to stay safe is to engage in scary play, which helps them understand threats.

Not only are kids curious about threats, they also have evolved in a world where things weren't as easy and safe as they are now. Kids have had to face many of the same challenges that adults had to face during our evolutionary history, and kids also had to face a bunch of challenges many adults didn't, given their obvious vulnerabilities. A young child who can't take care of themself is going to be in a far more precarious position in a disaster than a fully able adult.

We worry about our kids being safe, but we also worry about how they will learn all the things they need to know to succeed in society. The pandemic disruption to their education was just the latest, biggest worry. Even before the pandemic, there were challenges around the expectations of our educational systems, challenges I remember having in elementary and middle school. I was bored and unmotivated. So I get the millions of kids who struggle to sit in their seats and just listen to adults lecture at them for eight hours a day.

EMPOWERING THE NEXT GENERATION

If we can set up cooperative and collaborative learning spaces where kids' fundamental (and morbid!) curiosity can be piqued, this can allow learning to happen more organically so that kids will be much more engaged. Then institutions of higher learning can become much more generative spaces where students can participate in helping find solutions while learning simultaneously.

If we can create learning opportunities that involve joy and play, youngsters will not only remember the material better but also be able to apply it more readily because they will have practiced applying it through fun and games.

It's not just young people who should be empowered to play and engage in these ways; everyone should be empowered to create, teach, learn, share. In short, we need to empower the next generation to get the knowledge they need (from educators, their environments, and each other) and also empower them to experiment with new structures and approaches so that we can all do a better job managing risk. Youth are the hope for the future. And, thankfully, they (by and large) want to create and share and learn.

Let's also not forget that young people have a lot to teach, and that sometimes they are the ones who are able to jump into action during a catastrophe while adults can have more trouble. This is exactly what happened in Mati, Greece, in the aftermath of the devastating fire we talked about on page 168. But what is truly astounding about these young people is that they now travel around Greece to areas that have been hit by fires to help those communities recover. They are intrinsically motivated to share their knowledge far and wide. They see that there is a need and they know that they have what it takes to help, and so they go, on their own time and at their own expense, to help strangers who are trying to piece their lives and communities back together after destruction. They are true teachers of resilience and exemplars of cooperation.

There's a lot to be optimistic about when we look at how youth are handling these challenging days. For example, the Sunrise Movement is a group of activists under thirty-five taking action on climate change. And that's just one example; many young people are seeking out education and career trajectories based on improving people's lives and managing the existential risks that we are facing. These young people seem particularly adept at embracing the reality of the risks we are facing and moving toward action.

ENJOY THE END OF TIMES, EMBRACE THE NEW TIMES
Working to make the world more unfucked starts with prepping for yourself and your loved ones by assessing your

unique vulnerabilities. What are the kinds of disasters that are common in your neck of the woods or swath of desert? What do you need to have on hand to be ready to deal with them? Who in your immediate network is more vulnerable than you? What can you do to help them be safe in the event of a disaster? After you assess your situation, then you can start prepping. Not full-on doomsday style (unless you're into that, and then sure), but prepping for the kinds of emergencies that are likely to hit you and your loved ones.

> Embracing the apocalypse gives us an opportunity to change, grow, and find ways to thrive in the chaos and uncertainty of everything.

In the process of prepping, if you do it right, you will be learning more about your region and yourself. You'll actually gather the information about the kinds of disasters that are likely to happen, and you'll have a plan for what to do in the event of the most likely emergencies. By being ready, even on a small scale, you'll lower your stress about the possibility that shit will hit the fan tomorrow.

The key to thriving in the apocalypse is to make apocalypse preparation and response social and fun. You can do this by sharing *A Field Guide to the Apocalypse* with others (there are plenty of apocalypse book clubs out there), and building a community of preparedness among your friends, neighbors, coworkers, and family. Together, we can embrace the fun of practical prepping and managing risk collectively, working together to raise the next generation of apocalypse-resilient young people.

Yes, the apocalypse is here, in the sense that the risk inherent in the world has been revealing itself, heralding the beginning of a new era where we cannot ignore the reality of the disasters and catastrophes all around us. This is an opportunity for us to re-envision the world that we share, to embrace our new apocalypse-ready selves, and to support the communities that are ready to work together to manage the risks of our increasingly uncertain times.

Embracing the apocalypse gives us an opportunity to change, grow, and find ways to thrive in the chaos and uncertainty of everything. We can embrace reality, no matter how apocalyptic, knowing that we will work together to solve our many problems, be there for each other in times of need, and learn to thrive as individuals and communities despite the many challenges we face.

We started at the end, so it's only appropriate that we end at the beginning: the beginning of a new era where everything is fine, not because we deny reality but because we embrace the apocalypse as an opportunity to learn, grow, and thrive together in these wild times. So, let's make some new friends, face the reality of how fucked up a lot of things are, and go in for that apocalypse win by embracing the new times we're living in with a spirit of cooperation, curiosity, and playful imagination. Because these qualities in the face of our challenges are central to our very humanity. So, don't fret. This is just the beginning.

SOURCES

For a complete, unabridged notes list with links, please visit: Workman.com/Apocalypse

CHAPTER ONE

Page 2: Donovan L. Mathias, "NASA Asteroid Impact Risk Assessment," February 27, 2018.

Pages 4–5: Various revolutions, Encyclopedia Britannica, last updated June 4, 2023.

Page 10: Tony Phillips, "Why the World Didn't End Yesterday," NASA Science, accessed June 23, 2023.

Page 12: Texas Veterinary Medical Association, "World Zoonoses Day: Most Emerging Infectious Diseases Originate in Animals," *Infection Control Today*, November 14, 2020.

Page 14: D. Gurven and Raziel J. Davison, "Periodic Catastrophes over Human Evolutionary History Are Necessary to Explain the Forager Population Paradox," *PNAS* (June 10, 2019).

Page 15: L. Cronk et al., "Managing Risk through Cooperation: Need-Based Transfers and Risk Pooling Among the Societies of the Human Generosity Project," in *Global Perspectives on Long Term Community Resource Management: Studies in Human Ecology and Adaptation*, ed. L. R. Lozny and T. H. McGovern, vol. 11 (Springer, Cham, 2019).

Page 16: L. Cronk and A. Aktipis, "Design Principles for Risk-Pooling Systems," *Nature Human Behavior* 5 (2021): 825–33.

CHAPTER TWO

Page 22: Casey Henley, *Foundations of Neuroscience* (East Lansing: Michigan State University Libraries, 2021).

Page 31: J. Tooby and I. DeVore, "The Reconstruction of Hominid Behavioral Evolution Through Strategic Modeling," in *The Evolution of Human Behavior: Primate Models*, ed. Warren G. Kinzey (1987).

Kim Hill and A. Magdalena Hurtado, "Cooperative Breeding in South American Hunter-Gatherers," *Proceedings of the Royal Society B: Biological Sciences* 276, no. 1674 (2009): 3863–70.

Pages 34–35: C. M. Allison, K. Roggensack, and A.B. Clarke, "Highly Explosive Basaltic Eruptions Driven by CO_2 Exsolution," *Nature Communications* 12, no. 217 (2021).

"The 15 Most Dangerous Active Volcanoes in the World," *Popular Mechanics*, February 14, 2022.

Trevor English, "A Close Look at the 9 Most Active Volcanoes in the World," Interesting Engineering, March 17, 2023.

Page 37: Robert Kurzban and C. Athena Aktipis, "Modularity and the Social Mind: Are Psychologists too Selfish?," *Personality and Social Psychology Review* 11, no. 2 (2007): 131–49.

Page 39: Lutz Greisiger, "Apocalypticism, Millenarianism, and Messianism," in *The Oxford Handbook of the Abrahamic Religions*, ed. Moshe Blidstein, Adam J. Silverstein, and Guy G. Stroumsa (Oxford and New York: Oxford University Press, 2015), 272–94, doi:10.1093/oxfordhb/9780199697762.013.14.

Page 43: "Preparedness 101: Zombie Pandemic," US Centers for Disease Control.

Page 44: "CONPLAN 8888," U.S. Strategic Command, CONPLAN_8888-11.pdf, accessed August 8, 2023.

Page 48: Coltan Scrivner, "The Psychology of Morbid Curiosity: Development and Initial Validation of the Morbid Curiosity Scale," *Personality and Individual Differences* 183 (2021): 111139.

Page 50: L. S. Berk et al., "Modulation of Neuroimmune Parameters during the Eustress of Humor-Associated Mirthful Laughter," *Alternative Therapy Health Medicine* 7 (2001): 62–72.

Page 56: Andy Norman, *Mental Immunity: Infectious Ideas, Mind-Parasites, and the Search for a Better Way to Think* (New York: Harper Wave, 2021).

D. Smith et al., "Cooperation and the Evolution Of Hunter-Gatherer Storytelling," *Nature Communication* 8, no. 1853 (2017).

Page 57: D. G. Dutton and A. P. Aron, "Some Evidence for Heightened Sexual Attraction under Conditions of High Anxiety," *Journal of Personality and Social Psychology* 30, no. 4 (1974): 510–17.

Cathryn Townsend, Athena Aktipis, and Lee Cronk, "Does Scarcity Lead to Selfishness?," *Anthropology News* (May/June 2021).

Page 58: D. T. Kenrick and R. B. Cialdini, "Romantic Attraction: Misattribution Versus Reinforcement Explanations," *Journal of Personality and Social Psychology* 35, no. 6 (1977): 381–91.

Page 61: Casey Henley, *Foundations of Neuroscience* (East Lansing: Michigan State University Libraries, 2021).

Page 63: Michelle D. H. de Haan, Iroise Dumontheil, and Mark H. Johnson, *Developmental Cognitive Neuroscience: An Introduction*, 5th ed. (Wiley-Blackwell, 2023).

Page 69: Athena Aktipis and Diego Guevara Beltran, "Can Some Microbes Promote Host Stress and Benefit Evolutionarily from this Strategy?," *BioEssays* 43, no. 1 (2021): 2000188.

Page 72: Robert M. Sapolsky, *Why Zebras Don't Get Ulcers: The Acclaimed Guide to Stress, Stress-Related Diseases, and Coping*, 3rd ed. (New York: Macmillan, 2004).

Page 75: Melissa B. Manus, "Evolutionary Mismatch," *Evolution, Medicine, and Public Health* 1, (2018): 190–91.

CHAPTER THREE

Page 85: L. Cronk et al., "Managing Risk Through Cooperation: Need-Based Transfers and Risk Pooling Among the Societies of the Human Generosity Project," *Studies in Human Ecology and Adaptation*, vol. 11, June 22, 2019.

Page 87: L. Cronk et al., "A Solidarity-Type World: Need-Based Helping among Ranchers in the Southwestern United States," *Human Nature* 32, 482–508, 2021.

Diego Guevara Beltran, Denise Mercado, Jessica D. Ayers, Andrew Van Horn, Joe Alcock, Peter M. Todd, Lee Cronk, and Athena Aktipis, "Unpredictable Needs Are Associated with Lower Expectations of Repayment," *Current Research in Ecological and Social Psychology* 4 (2023): 100095.

Page 90: M. Campennì, L. Cronk, and A. Aktipis, "Need-Based Transfers Enhance Resilience to Shocks: An Agent-Based Model of a Maasai Risk Pooling System," *Human Ecology* 50, 35-48, 2022.

Page 95: "The Health Benefits of Volunteering: A Review of Recent Research," AmeriCorps, 2007.

Pages 96–97: Daniel Gerszon Mahler, Nishant Yonzan, Ruth Hill, Christoph Lakner, Haoyu Wu, and Nobuo Yoshida, "Pandemics, prices, and poverty," *World Bank Blogs*, April 13, 2022.

"List of Famines," *Wikipedia*, last modified June 20, 2023.

"UN Food Chief Warns of 'Hell on Earth' Food Shortages," *Associated Press*, September 22, 2021.

Hannah Duggal and Mohammed Haddad, "Infographic: Russia, Ukraine and the Global Wheat Supply," *Al Jazeera*, February 17, 2022.

Darryl Fears, "A Mega-Drought Will Grip U.S. in the Coming Decades, NASA Researchers Say," *The Washington Post*, February 12, 2015.

"The Global Maize Market Snapshot in June 2021," *Food and Agriculture Organization of the United Nations*, June 2021.

"World Food Situation," *Food and Agriculture Organization of the United Nations*, February 6, 2023.

"UN Food Chief: Billions Needed to Avert Unrest, Starvation," *Associated Press, Voice of America Science and Health*, April 1, 2023.

Romina Ruiz-Goiriena, "More Americans struggling to put food on the table after federal benefits end," *USA Today*, updated September 27, 2021.

Page 98: Aaron D. Lightner, Anne C. Pisor, Edward H. Hagen, "In Need-Based Sharing, Sharing Is More Important Than Need," *Evolution and Human Behavior* (2023).

Jessica D. Ayers, Jaimie Arona Krems, and Athena Aktipis, "A Factor Analytic Examination of Women's and Men's Friendship Preferences," *Personality and Individual Differences* 206 (2023): 112120.

Page 99: Randolph M. Nesse, ed., *Evolution and the Capacity for Commitment* (Russell Sage Foundation, 2001).

Page 100: A. Aktipis, "Know When to Walk Away: Contingent Movement and the Evolution of Cooperation," *Journal of Theoretical Biology*, 231(2): 249–60, November 21, 2004.

Page 101: Ronald Noë and Peter Hammerstein, "Biological Markets: Supply and Demand Determine the Effect of Partner Choice in Cooperation, Mutualism and Mating," *Behavioral Ecology and Sociobiology* 35, no. 1 (1994): 1–11.

Page 103: A. Aktipis et al., "Understanding Cooperation through Fitness Interdependence," *Nature Human Behavior* 2 (2018): 429–31.

Page 106: J. Tooby and L. Cosmides, "Friendship and the Banker's Paradox: Other Pathways to the Evolution of Adaptations for Altruism," in *Evolution of Social Behaviour Patterns in Primates and Man*, ed. W. G. Runciman, J. M. Smith, and R. I. M. Dunbar (Oxford University Press, 1996), 119–43.

Page 107: Rebecca Solnit, *A Paradise Built in Hell: The Extraordinary Communities that Arise in Disaster* (New York: Penguin, 2010).

Page 108: Lee Clarke and Caron Chess, "Elites and Panic: More to Fear than Fear Itself," *Social Forces* 87, no. 2 (December 2008): 993–1014.

Page 109: "Voices from the Future | Greg Kochanowski," Arizona State University, August 1, 2020.

Page 110: R. Axelrod and W. D. Hamilton, "The Evolution of Cooperation," *Science* 211, no. 4489, (March 27, 1981): 1390–96, doi:10.1126/science.7466396, PMID: 7466396.

Page 112: B. Skyrms, *The Stag Hunt and the Evolution of Social Structure* (Cambridge: Cambridge University Press, 2003), doi:10.1017/CBO9781139165228.

Page 114: John Maynard Smith and David Harper, *Animal Signals* (Oxford University Press, 2003).

Diekmann, "Volunteer's Dilemma," *Journal of Conflict Resolution* 29, no. 4 (1985): 605–10.

Page 118: R. Schuessler, "The Gradual Decline of Cooperation: Endgame Effects in Evolutionary Game Theory," *Theory and Decision* 26 (1989): 133–55.

CHAPTER FOUR

Page 127: Gayle Spinazze, "Press Release: Doomsday Clock Set at 90 Seconds to Midnight," *Bulletin of the Atomic Scientists*, January 24, 2023.

Tom Nichols, "Five Ways a Nuclear War Could Still Happen." *National Interest*, June 16, 2014.

Page 128: Michael Dobbs, "Cuban Missile Crisis: How Close America Came to Nuclear War With Russia: Archival Information about the Cuban Missile Crisis Shows Just How Close We Came to Nuclear Armageddon," History Net, June 13, 2022.

"Plan A," Princeton University Program on Science & Global Security, accessed June 21, 2023.

Page 130: Brendan Cole, "Vladimir Putin Has Threatened Nuclear War at Least 35 Times— U.K.'s Johnson," *Newsweek*, July 1, 2022.

Page 131: "Solar System Exploration: Our Galactic Neighborhood: Beyond Our Solar System," NASA, April 20, 2023.

"How Many Habitable Planets Are Out There?," SETI Institute, October 29, 2020.

Page 133: M. Wheelis, "Biological Warfare at the 1346 Siege of Caffa," *Emerging Infectious Diseases* 8, no. 9 (2002): 971–75.

Page 134: "DIY Bacterial Gene Engineering CRISPR Kit," The Odin, accessed June 12, 2023.

"Volume Five: Anthrax at Sverdlovsk, 1979: U.S. Intelligence on the Deadliest Modern Outbreak," *National Security Archive Electronic Briefing Book No. 61*, ed. Robert A. Wampler and Thomas S. Blanton (November 15, 2001), accessed June 21, 2023.

Page 135: Cristi Kempf, "U.S. Is, Unwilling or Incapable, of Learning the Real Lessons of the Pandemic, *Atlantic* Journalist Argues," *UChicago News*, November 8, 2022.

Page 137: Luc Olinga, "Elon Musk Says a Tesla Catgirl Robot Is Coming," *The Street*, October 1, 2022.

Page 140: Alex Kerai, "2023 Cell Phone Usage Statistics: Mornings Are for Notifications," Reviews.org, May 9, 2023.

Rachel Metz, "Smartphones Are Weapons of Mass Manipulation, and This Guy Is Declaring War on Them," *MIT Technology Review*, October 19, 2017.

Pages 142–143: Ann Gibbons, "Are We in the Middle of a Sixth Mass Extinction?," *Science*, March 2, 2011.

WWF Australia, "New WWF Report: 3 Billion Animals Impacted by Australia's Bushfire Crisis." July 27, 2020.

Alex Migdal, "More Than a Billion Seashore Animals May Have Cooked to Death in B.C. Heat Wave, Says UBC Researcher," *CBC News*, July 5, 2021.

Page 144: Marina Manoukian, "The Tragic True Story of the 2003 European Heat Wave," *Grunge*, July 30, 2022.

Emily Senesac, "Great Chicago Heat Wave of 1995," National Weather Service Heritage, accessed June 12, 2023.

"Potentially Fatal Combinations of Humidity and Heat Are Emerging across the Globe," Earth Institute at Columbia University, May 20, 2020.

Page 145: Trent Koss, "Humans Have Dramatically Increased Extent, Duration of Wildfire Season," *CU Boulder Today*, February 27, 2017.

Page 146: Helena Smith, "'In My Nightmares I'm Always in the Sea': A Year on from the Greek Fires," *The Guardian*, July 20, 2019.

Reuters, "Aftermath of Greece's 'Armageddon' Fire," July 27, 2018.

Page 148: Matt Williams, "Will Earth Survive When the Sun Becomes a Red Giant?," *Universe Today*, May 10, 2016.

Page 154: L. Cronk et al., "Managing Risk through Cooperation: Need-Based Transfers and Risk Pooling Among the Societies of the Human Generosity Project," in *Global Perspectives on Long Term Community Resource Management: Studies in Human Ecology and Adaptation*, ed. L. R. Lozny and T. H. McGovern, vol. 11 (Springer, Cham, 2019).

Page 166: Ed Yong, "We're Already Barreling toward the Next Pandemic," *The Atlantic*, September 29, 2021.

Pages 169–170: L. Cronk et al., "'A Solidarity-Type World': Need-Based Helping among Ranchers in the Southwestern United States," *Human Nature* 32 (2021): 482–508.

Page 171: David T. Beito, *From Mutual Aid to the Welfare State: Fraternal Societies and Social Services*, 1890–1967 (Chapel Hill: University of North Carolina Press, 2000).

Page 175: Keith G. Tidball and Marianne E. Krasny, "Introduction: Greening in the Red Zone," in *Greening in the Red Zone: Disaster, Resilience, and Community Greening*, ed. Keith G. Tidball and Marianne E. Krasny (Netherlands: Springer, 2013), 3–24.

Page 178: Athena Aktipis and Keith G. Tidball, "How Each of Us Can Prepare for the Next Pandemic," *Scientific American*, May 11, 2021.

CHAPTER FIVE

Page 185: Emily St. John Mandel, *Station Eleven* (New York: Knopf, 2014).

Page 195: Emily Zarka, "Duct Tape Before Guns: Emily Zarka," *Zombified: Your Source for Fresh Brains*, produced and directed by Athena Aktipis and Dave Lundberg-Kenrick, July 30, 2019.

Page 209: Korea National Heritage Preservation Agency, "Tradition of Kimchi-Making in the Democratic People's Republic of Korea," *UNESCO Silk Roads Programme*, 2013, accessed June 25, 2023.

Page 211: Mathew Sandoval, "How Commercialization over the Centuries Transformed the Day of the Dead," *The Conversation*, October 27, 2021.

ACKNOWLEDGMENTS

I have many people to thank for the fact that I've managed to survive writing a book about the apocalypse. I must start with my Zombified Media Z-Team. Thank you to Joe Alcock, Cristina Baciu, Jessica Brinkworth, Cameron Carlson, Liz Grumbach, Nicole Hudson, Dave Lundberg-Kenrick, Mzilikaze Koné, Erica O'Neil, Ilana Rein, Pam Winfrey, and Emily Zarka for being by my side through the revelation of risk that has been these last few years.

Thank you to all the friends and colleagues who read early drafts of this manuscript, gave feedback, and otherwise contributed thinking from their delicious brains. Especially to Steven Beschloss, Lee Cronk, Gary Dirks, Mark Flinn, Ed Finn, Jeremy Koster, Andrew Maynard, Denise Mercado, Erica O'Neil, Dianne Price, Coltan Scrivner, Keith Tidball, and Peter Todd. And thanks to all the guests who have generously shared their brains with me on my *Zombified* and *Channel Zed* podcasts over the years.

Thank you to Jeff Shreve, the best agent anybody could ever ask for, and the crew at Workman: my editor John Meils, phenomenal layout designer Rae Ann Spitzenberger, and everyone working behind the scenes, including Barbara Peragine and Kimberly Ehart. Thank you, Neil Smith, for bringing this fun apocalyptic world to life with your amazing illustrations. This book is really the work of our shared brains and a labor of soul-consuming love for the apocalypse.

Deepest gratitude to my mom, Helga, and my dad, Stelios. Mom, you taught me to never be afraid to fail, to nurture creativity at all costs, and to savor failures as our best opportunities for learning. Dad, you taught me to push against unnecessary constraints, challenge rules that need challenging, and to find my own path.

The path that brought me to this book was filled with teachers all along the way who encouraged me, educated me, and challenged me to be my best self, including Vicky Edwards, Joy Joyce, Rob Kurzban, Will Nifong, Noelwah Netusil, Allen Neuringer, Ed Raddatz, and Mel Rutherford.

For being there for me during the apocalyptic moments that I've personally experienced as I've been writing this book, I have to thank Martie Haselton, Nicole Hess, Sarah Hill, Andreas Kropf, and Barbara Natterson-Horowitz. And thank you to everyone who has been a support in my children's lives while I wrote this book, especially Carlo Maley, Veronica Mata, and Josh Warner.

A lively thanks to my music people: Julie Sullivan Brace, Annie Sorrel, Jerry Green, Mike McBeath, Baba Brinkman, my Flagstaff bluegrass jam crew, my FAMI fam, and everyone I've ever been in a jam circle with, for teaching me about the power of music for bringing people together, creating joy, and helping us thrive in the apocalypse.

A deeply unhinged thank you to all the people who taught me to be willing to take risks, to thrive in chaos without being an agent of it, to cultivate an adventuresome spirit, to climb things that scare me, to learn useful survival skills, and to not be afraid to try to fix my own house: Molly Odell, Evan Johnson, Charlie Brister (wherever you are), Sean Fa'asamala, Chris McCarthy, Keith Tidball (yes, again), Joe Alcock (yes, also again), and of course, Jake Blackwell.

Thank you to my kids, Avanna, Monty, and Vaughn, for all the things you have taught me about love, survival, and of course, memes. I would be much less informed and much more boring if you didn't take me under your wise young wings and patiently explain to me what is happening in the world of digital cultural transmission.

And thank you to all my students for challenging my assumptions and inviting me to look at the world through fresh eyes, for making me laugh, for being willing to play, and for being honest with me about your struggles to make sense of the world and find your place in it. You hold the pen to write the next chapter in our ofttimes apocalyptic human story. No pressure or anything.

INDEX

A

adaptation of humans for apocalypse, 6–10, 17, 27–36, 76
airline travel, 202–3
alien invasion, 130–33
all-hazards prepping, 43–44, 81, 129, 153–55, 174, 184, 195
alloparent, 228
amygdala, 25–27
antifragile systems, 168–69
anxious doom-scroller persona, 191
apocalypse-casual lifestyle, 183–224
  community building and, 206–8
  different approaches to, 189–91
  fashion and, 184, 187–88, 194–95
  fun and weird culture in, 208–24
  at home, 195–96
  mindset and, 194
  on the road, 197–206
apocalypse-core persona, 189
"apocalypse," use of word, 5–6
apocalyptic thinking, 39
Apocalypticus V: Road to Ruin, United Kingdom, 216
apocalyp*tish* times, embracing lifestyle shift in, 186–89
artificial intelligence (AI), 137–42
asteroids, 2
atmospheric rivers, 193

B

babies:
  go-bags for, 162
  human cooperation and, 31–33
back-to-the-lander persona, 190
being your best self, 224–27
Big One(s), defined, 126
biological warfare, 133–34
boat safety, 203–4
brain, 21–27, 30–31
Burning Man, 58, 214

C

cancer, viii, 138
car kits, 120, 153, 154, 163, 165, 174, 192, 208
Centers for Disease Control, 43–44
cheating, 80, 98, 99, 111, 118, 170, 172–73, 174–75
Chicken, game of, 129, 130
children, 228–30
  apocalypse parties for, 212–17
  human cooperation and, 31–33
  learning opportunities for, 229–30
  small, go-bags for, 162
cleaning and hygiene supplies, 159
climate change, 3, 11–13, 29–31, 39, 97, 126, 142–47, 193, 230
  fires and, 126, 142, 143, 145–47
  WetBulb death and, 143–44
clothing, apocalypse-casual style and, 184, 187–88, 194–95
clusterfuck apocalypse, 1, 19, 125–26, 128, 135–37, 143
cognitive immune system, 56
cognitive niche, 30–31
Cold War, 128–29
commitment theory, 99–100
communication, humans built for, 33
community, 98, 116, 192, 217
  apocalypse-ready, building, 8, 17, 181, 206–9, 231
  benefits of being helpful within, 119, 120–21
  greening after disasters and, 175–76
  having babies and, 31–33
  information sources for, 33, 176
  risk management and, 84, 85, 147–48, 165–72, 175–79, 181, 185
cooperation:
  as central feature of human life, 36
  cultivating, 172–81
  large-scale societies and, 118
  see also need-based transfer systems; Z-teams
cooperative extension programs, 174, 176–77, 178, 179, 207